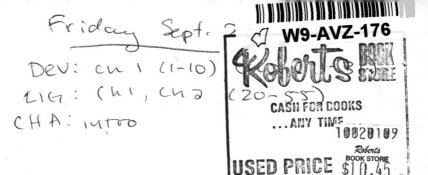
Chasing After Street Gangs

MASTERS SERIES IN CRIMINOLOGY

Series Editor
Henry N. Pontell
School of Social Ecology, University of California, Irvine

White-Collar and Corporate Crime
by Gilbert Geis

Electronic Crime
by Peter Grabosky

Chasing After Street Gangs: A Forty-Year Journey
by Malcolm W. Klein

FORTHCOMING

Feminist Criminology: Crime, Patriarchy,
and the Control of Women
by Meda Chesney-Lind

The Great Punishment Experiment
by Todd R. Clear

Social Support and Crime in America:
A New Criminology
by Francis T. Cullen

Social Roots of Crime: Why Some Societies Are
More Violent Than Others
by Elliott Currie

Developmental and Life Course Theories of Offending
by David P. Farrington

Crimes of Memory
by Elizabeth Loftus

Identity Fraud
by Henry N. Pontell

MASTERS SERIES
IN CRIMINOLOGY

Malcolm W. Klein

Chasing After
Street Gangs

A Forty-Year Journey

PEARSON
Prentice
Hall

UPPER SADDLE RIVER, NEW JERSEY 07458

Library of Congress Cataloging-in-Publication Data
Klein, Malcolm W.
    Chasing after street gangs : a forty-year journey / Malcolm W. Klein.
    p. cm.—(Masters series in criminology)
    Includes bibliographical references and index.
    ISBN 0-13-170948-8
    1. Gangs—United States. 2. Gangs—Europe. I. Title. II. Series.
    HV6439.U5K582 2007
    364.106'6—dc22

                                                    2006016915

Editor-in-Chief: Vernon R. Anthony
Marketing Manager: Adam Kloza
Assistant Editor: Mayda Bosco
Editorial Assistant: Jillian Allison
Production Management: GGS Book
    Services
Production Editor: Trish Finley
Production Liaison: Barbara Marttine
    Cappuccio

**Director of Manufacturing and
    Production:** Bruce Johnson
Managing Editor: Mary Carnis
Manufacturing Manager: Ilene Sanford
Manufacturing Buyer: Cathleen Petersen
Senior Design Coordinator: Mary Siener
Interior Design: Lisa Klausing
Cover Designer: Brian Kane
Printer/Binder: R.R. Donnelley & Sons
    Company

Pearson Education LTD
Pearson Education Singapore, Pte. Ltd
Pearson Education, Canada, Ltd
Pearson Education–Japan
Pearson Education Australia PTY, Limited
Pearson Education North Asia Ltd
Pearson Educación de Mexico, S.A. de C.V.
Pearson Education Malaysia, Pte. Ltd

10 9 8 7 6 5 4 3 2 1
ISBN 0-13-170948-8

This book is dedicated to sociologist James F. Short, anthropologist Walter B. Miller, and social worker Irving A. Spergel, three pioneers of modern gang research whose careers have provided the continuity of knowledge so lacking in much of the field. The book is my attempt to extend their tradition of continuity. By the time I started my career in the mid-1960s, Short, Miller, and Spergel were already establishing the paths for the rest of us to follow. That's what pioneers do.

I am grateful to six excellent scholars and teachers for their critical comments on an early draft of this treatise. These younger pioneers are Margaret Gatz, Charles Katz, Cheryl Maxson, Jody Miller, Dana Peterson, and Tom Ward.

CONTENTS

"All parents damage their children," said writer Mitch Albom.[1] But it's reciprocal, isn't it? Many children damage their parents, mostly because parents have expectations, hopes, and desires that their children often cannot fulfill and may not even recognize. We can extend this notion: Many communities damage their children, and many children in turn do harm to their communities.

In perhaps no setting is all this more true than that of street gang members, their families, and their communities. The reciprocal damage in the world of street gangs is both direct and collateral, widespread and occasionally severe; this is now far more true than it was some decades ago. And we haven't done much about it, at least not successfully. Why is this the case? Why, when eighty years have passed since Frederic Thrasher introduced gangs to the worlds of research, policy, and practice, are we not further along in melding our increasing knowledge with expanding options in practice? The reasons are numerous: let me suggest some of these.

1. The number of scholars who have stayed genuinely engaged in gang research and policy throughout their careers can be counted on

one hand. I count myself as one of these, and Jim Short, Walter Miller, and Irv Spergel as the others, as noted in the dedication in this book. I've been at it since 1962, and the others for even longer. With the bulk of gang research having taken place only within the last two decades or so, a lot of wheels have been reinvented, slowing the pace of progress.

2. Gang research can be very taxing, variously so depending on the research methods employed. This is especially true of street research. Thus, hanging in is the exception, not the rule. Two or three years of intensive fieldwork with gang members and their neighborhoods are quite enough for most who try it. You're on your own; long hours with the gang remove you from your own family; your efforts are seldom appreciated by the gangs, their families, the police, or the community; if you have expectations for reliable and reciprocal collaborations with gang members, you will be continually frustrated; and it gets cold out there on the streets—and occasionally a bit dangerous. Additionally, few field researchers can afford the time to study more than one or two gangs, thus leaving in question whether what they learn is generic or unique to those one or two situations.

3. Different research methods often yield different "knowledge" about gangs. Those who gather their gang data from police and court files soon learn how biased, unevenly available, and limited these official records of gang crime are, to say nothing of the character of gang members and their settings. Those who gather interview or questionnaire data from gang members or their families suffer fewer personal hardships than field researchers, but they are forever doomed to question the validity of the responses they elicit. Like their colleagues using police files, they also lack exposure to the direct lives of gang members that gives special value to field research.

Police file analysts and survey researchers, however, are less limited to one gang or one site and thus may claim more generalizable findings: breadth instead of depth. Ideally, of course, one would hope for a combination of methods so that one could triangulate on "truth" (whatever that might be). The researchers most likely to achieve this—like the researchers mentioned in the dedication, along with some others—are those who expose themselves to gang intervention programs whose evaluations require a multiplicity of methods in order to assess the success and increase the value of such programs. But here the frustrations of each method may accumulate and be augmented by the pains of collaboration between researcher and practitioner. If one reads the stories of such collaborations offered by Miller (1958), Spergel (1966), Klein (1971), and Fearn, Decker, and Curry (2001), it is a wonder that any of them would continue in such work.

4. And then there is the question of how much gang knowledge is enough. At what point can a writer about gangs, like me, say, "Okay, I know enough now to instruct others" or—more frighteningly—"I know enough now to suggest what policies and practices should be launched to reduce gang problems"?

I started my journey in October 1962 in total ignorance of the gang world. I had never taken a course in criminology, only one in sociology and one in anthropology, and none in child development or adolescence or family studies. Seemingly, I was the worst possible choice as a recruit into gang research. One strength, though, impelled me toward accepting the challenge. I was trained as a social psychologist; I had useful exposure to the nature of groups (gangs, after all, are groups), social attitudes and perceptions, leadership, social communications, race relations, and social class issues. After attending my very first (and rather contentious) gang member gathering, I saw much of my formal academic training playing out in front of me. Gangs weren't a mystery, I told myself; they're merely an extreme case of what I had already studied for years.

And so I was primed, although I certainly had no idea that the new journey would last for over four decades. To jump-start my trip, I traveled from Los Angeles to Boston, New York, and Chicago to interview and learn from experts already intensely engaged in gang research, people like Walter Miller, Lloyd Ohlin, Rita Simon, Irving Spergel, Jim Short, Bob Gordon, Henry McKay, Solomon Kobrin, Gerry Suttles, and Hans Mattick. I completed my travels during the winter of 1962–1963; it was bitterly cold, and yet gang members were out on the street. I found this quite amazing, but Hans Mattick explained what it is like for youth who feel marginalized and alienated, seeking company and identity and status where they could best find it— among themselves, away from the constraints of adult supervision. The street (literally and figuratively) is where this fellowship develops and thrives, bitter cold weather or not.

Mattick gave me an evening I've never forgotten. A large, gruff man with a history of social activism, he first sat me down at his office and attempted to answer my many naïve questions about gangs and gang communities. He then invited me to his home that same evening. While his indulgent wife cooked us up a magnificent dinner, Mattick shoved me into his home library and gave me a one-hour, uninterrupted lecture about everything I needed to know, pointing his finger at this book and that book to indicate how much reading I had to do, and fast! I was a captive in his world, no less than a con in his prison cell. When I was finally released for what might have seemed like my last supper, he then capped it all off with his memorable (and only) supportive comment: "Within six months, you'll know all there is to know about gangs."

Well, in this at least, Hans Mattick was dead wrong. Here I am, more than forty years later, still learning more about gangs. It ain't easy: Why do I still have things to learn? Why do my fellow criminologists still have things to learn? And why, therefore, must the readers of this book suspend their current understandings of street gangs and follow the long journey to new understandings? Let me suggest a dozen reasons:

1. Over the past forty years and more, certain important aspects of American street gangs have changed, although their basic nature has not. We must be alert to changes in gang prevalence, size, gender and ethnicity, crime patterns, and the like. Yesterday's knowledge is not good enough.[2]

2. Gang studies—more accurately, gang researchers—have lacked coordination of their efforts. Thus, *comparative* research has not been common, and it is comparisons that yield generalized knowledge. There have been too few comparisons between gang and non-gang youth, between gangs and non-gang groups, between different—and different *kinds* of—gangs, between gang communities (neighborhoods, cities, countries), between historical periods over the last half century, and between the different impressions of gangs one gets from different research methods (e.g., observation, ethnography, youth surveys, and archival research in police, court, and correctional files). I have expanded on this in a recent article (Klein, 2005).

3. Consensus on a definition of street gangs has not been achieved, although in Section 2 of this book I will offer a definition that seems to satisfy most needs. Until this or some other definition achieves general acceptance, we will not know with any certainty that our "gang knowledge" is in fact a valid achievement. Suppose I report that all sports teams can be defined similarly: Does that satisfy you that the definition will apply equally to basketball, baseball, football, track, field hockey, and equestrian teams?

4. There has been, until recently, too much reliance on case studies of individual gangs, whether done by street observation, ethnography, or survey methods. Each gang, as a case, may have unique features that are not recognized as such because the study stands alone, without

comparisons. Case-studied gangs need to be placed in a wide array of gangs so that we can derive general observations of gangs as a *class* of phenomena.

5. Too little attention has been paid to the specifically *group* nature of street gangs. There are group processes that drive gang behavior above and beyond the sum of individual behaviors, yet most gang research merely adds up the acts of the individual gang members. In addition, there are, we now know, discernibly different kinds of gangs based on their structural characteristics that should warn us against making unconsidered statements, such as all gangs are violent, gangs are heavily involved in drug trafficking, gangs appear in big cities, gangs are well organized, girls don't get much involved in gangs, and so on.

6. Too little attention has been paid to the communities in which gangs appear. Observing and understanding neighborhoods is far more complex than studying their gangs; yet it is communities that spawn gangs and must inevitably be the proximal focus for controlling them.

7. Gang research has too often been driven by the interests of government and private funding organizations. The result has been emphases based too often on politics and ideology, at the expense of theory and knowledge building. Gang prevention and amelioration were fostered by the funders in the 1950s and 1960s. By the early 1980s, the trend had shifted to gang control and suppression (where it remains today). One can see the shift in the sources of data used to measure gang activity, from field observations, ethnography, and gang member interviews in the earlier period to broad youth surveys and police data in the later period, from an earlier interest in the character of gangs to the later interest in gang crime specifically. *Gangs* have changed less than the alteration of gang research *methods* has suggested.

8. There has been too little research (especially in the United States, less so in Europe) on ongoing youth groups to which street gangs might

be compared. Most youth groups are not gangs, but the uniqueness of the gang would be clearer and better understood in the context of the more numerous and the more "normal" groups that young people generally form. Some readers of this book will feel that they were (or still are) members of groups that should be classified as gangs: Are their perceptions likely to be correct? I have maintained through much of my career that street gangs are caricatures of most adolescent and youth groups, that they are qualitatively different from most other groups.[3]

9. While there has been much research on the juvenile justice and juvenile welfare systems, little of it has deliberately incorporated the handling of gangs and gang matters. The need for special accommodations has not been tested for the most part, and the effect of the two systems on street gangs has not been assessed. Police departments, in particular, have proven very resistant to involvement in gang research and anti-gang program evaluations.

10. There has not been much appreciation of the interaction between the many types of methods (street observations, youth surveys, police data collection) used in gang research and the forms of knowledge they produce. And since most studies are carried out on different gangs, in different places, at different times, the combinations of methods and contexts often yield contrasting findings about how gangs form and are maintained, the sorts of people who join them, and the patterns of activities in which they engage. Choice of method is not random because researchers have their own preferences. The results of those choices do not readily yield generalizable knowledge.

11. When we review major programs of gang prevention, intervention, and suppression (and combinations of these) to determine what they have taught us about controlling the gang problem, we come upon a very discouraging situation: Most such programs have not been adequately implemented. We don't know what works, if anything, because

the program design and plans often fail to be established and maintained in the field.[4] Sometimes the plans are unrealistic; sometimes they are subverted by agency resistance and change; sometimes the field situation changes, requiring large changes in program plans and operations; sometimes personnel changes and new administrations result in different agendas. In any case, the original intention gets lost in practice. As a colleague once complained, MILTFP, 41—"Make It Like The Frigging Picture, For Once."

12. Closely tied to the last point is the common failure to implement an adequate and independent research evaluation of gang programs. There are a number of reasons for this: a lack of appreciation for what constitutes an adequate evaluation; anxiety that an independent evaluation will reflect poorly on the program; a lack of funding for an evaluation; mistakes in choosing competent evaluators; and the absence of reliable data that can yield a successful program evaluation. One can almost count on one hand the number of scientifically valid evaluations of gang programs; after some forty years of practice, this is a discouraging situation.

All the above might seem to be quite an indictment of the field of street gang research and practice, but I don't mean it to be. It is simply a compilation, in one essay, of how much is yet to be done. Although most gang control programs have been either inadequately implemented or not assessed, we don't need to throw out the baby with the bathwater. Many of these programs may have been helpful; it's just that we can't know which ones, or how helpful, without adequate research.

And as for the accumulation of knowledge about gangs, the faults listed above should not obscure the fact that we have gained a great deal of understanding about the nature of street gangs. The purpose of the following sections of this book is to demonstrate this gathering of information. Over time, we have indeed been "catching up" with gangs, learning much about them, and at least positioning ourselves to do something effective about them.

In Part 1, we will see some of the dominant trends emerging during the time of my forty-year journey through gang lands. In Part 2, we will delve more into the conceptual contexts that help us to understand those trends, both in knowledge accumulation and in approaches to gang control. Each section of Parts 1 and 2 will be short and compact, compressing the material to aid the reader. Concentrated reading is required to unpack it. The usual academic citations and references will be limited in order not to break up the flow of the narrative. However, a list of major summaries of gang research is offered for those who wish to delve more deeply into the often fascinating world of street gangs. At the end of each section, I have inserted a "Special Question," which can trigger discussion among the readers. Welcome to my world!

SPECIAL QUESTION: If gang research has proven so problematic, how might it be improved?

ENDNOTES

1. This sentiment appears in his sensitive and charming novel *The Five People You Meet in Heaven* (Hyperion, 2003).

2. A caution is in order here. Gang activity historically has shown both small and large cycles. There are ups and downs in the number of gangs, where they appear, how violent they are, and how they adopt special crime patterns such as drug distribution or auto theft. Our knowledge must spread over enough time that an upward or downward swing can be assessed as merely part of a pattern of cycles.

3. Section 2 of this book will speak directly to this point.

4. This issue had been broadly covered in Klein and Maxson, *Street Gang Patterns and Policies* (Oxford, England: Oxford University Press, 2006).

Chasing After Street Gangs

PART 1 | Four Levels of Street
Gang Information

SECTION 1 | GANG AND NON-GANG JURISDICTIONS

The four sections of Part 1 deal with four levels of gang information: where street gangs are located, how they compare with other groups, what kinds of youth they involve, and how their illegal behaviors are characterized. Common to all four sections are the pivotal issues of defining gangs, gang members, and gang crimes. We start with the question of where street gangs are found.

The first scientifically sound nationwide survey of street gang existence took place in 1996. Carried out by the newly established National Youth Gang Center (NYGC), the mailed survey went to a representative sample of 3,024 police and sheriffs' departments.[1] We're interested here in the returns from police departments in "larger" cities (over 25,000 people) and "small" cities (2,500 to 25,000 people). To begin our discussion, take a look at twenty-six cities in New York, the Empire State, the fabled land of that great musical theater about street gangs, *West Side Story*. From the list below, decide which cities you think emerged from the survey as those with active street gangs (all but four were "larger" cities).

NEW YORK STATE			
Albany ( )	Jamestown ( )	Perry ( )	Troy ( )
Auburn ( )	Manlius ( )	Poughkeepsie ( )	Utica ( )
Binghamton ( )	Mount Vernon ( )	Rochester ( )	Watertown ( )
Buffalo ( )	New Rochelle ( )	Schenectady ( )	White Plains ( )
Cicero ( )	New York City ( )	Scotia ( )	Yonkers ( )
Hempstead ( )	Orangetown ( )	South Nyack ( )	
Ithaca ( )	Oxford ( )	Syracuse ( )	

If you like, you can put pencil checks next to each city you think would have been a gang city in 1996—go ahead, it's your book. Obviously, New York City should be selected, but what about the others? Go ahead and guess; we'll get to the answers later.

Now do the same thing for a state from the heartland of the United States, Iowa. This list includes fourteen cities, all but one of which are in the "larger" category (over 25,000 people).

IOWA		
Ames ( )	Council Bluffs ( )	Mason City ( )
Bettendorf ( )	Davenport ( )	Sioux City ( )
Burlington ( )	Des Moines ( )	Urbandale ( )
Cedar Rapids ( )	Grinnell ( )	Waterloo ( )
Clinton ( )	Iowa City ( )	

Deciding which cities to check may be more difficult in the case of Iowa. These "larger" cities are not as large as a number of those in the

New York list. Still, the list is smaller and maybe this will make the guesses easier.

Finally, let's go to California, our most populous state and one with far more cities that might have gang problems. Everyone knows about Los Angeles, of course, but what about the rest of the Golden State? Our list includes 141 cities, most of which have 25,000 or more inhabitants. Here's a really tough test: to select which of these 141 jurisdictions reported having street gangs ("youth gangs" in the terminology of the NYGC). I doubt anyone really is familiar with 141 California cities, so take your time on this list. Make your best guesses and be prepared to get some right and some wrong.

CALIFORNIA				
Alameda ( )	Burbank ( )	Covina ( )	Firebaugh ( )	Inglewood ( )
Alhambra ( )	Campbell ( )	Crescent City ( )	Folsom ( )	Irvine ( )
Anaheim ( )	Carlsbad ( )	Cypress ( )	Fontana ( )	La Habra ( )
Antioch ( )	Cathedral City ( )	Daly City ( )	Fountain Valley ( )	La Verne ( )
Arcadia ( )	Ceres ( )	Davis ( )	Fremont ( )	Livermore ( )
Azusa ( )	Chico ( )	Delano ( )	Fresno ( )	Lodi ( )
Bakersfield ( )	Chino ( )	Dixon ( )	Fullerton ( )	Lompoc ( )
Baldwin Park ( )	Chula Vista ( )	Downey ( )	Garden Grove ( )	Long Beach ( )
Bell ( )	Claremont ( )	East Palo Alto ( )	Gardena ( )	Los Angeles ( )
Bell Gardens ( )	Clovis ( )	El Cajon ( )	Gilroy ( )	Los Barios ( )
Belmont ( )	Colton ( )	El Centro ( )	Half Moon Bay ( )	Los Gatos ( )
Berkeley ( )	Compton ( )	El Monte ( )	Hawthorne ( )	Madera ( )
Brea ( )	Concord ( )	Escondido ( )	Huntington Beach ( )	Manteca ( )
Brentwood ( )	Corona ( )	Eureka ( )	Huntington Park ( )	Maywood ( )
Buena Park ( )	Costa Mesa ( )	Farmersville ( )	Huron ( )	Menlo Park ( )

(*Continued*)

(*Continued*)

Merced ( )	Orange ( )	Riverside ( )	San Pablo ( )	Tustin ( )
Milpitas ( )	Oxnard ( )	Rohmert Park ( )	San Rafael ( )	Union City ( )
Monrovia ( )	Palm Springs ( )	Roseville ( )	Santa Ana ( )	Upland ( )
Montclair ( )	Paradise ( )	Sacramento ( )	Santa Barbara ( )	Vacaville ( )
Montebello ( )	Pittsburg ( )	Salinas ( )	Santa Clara ( )	Vallejo ( )
Monterey ( )	Placentia ( )	San Bernardino ( )	Santa Cruz ( )	Ventura ( )
Morgan Hill ( )	Pleasant Hill ( )	San Bruno ( )	Santa Paula ( )	Visalia ( )
Mountain View ( )	Porterville ( )	San Diego ( )	Santa Rosa ( )	Watsonville ( )
Napa ( )	Redding ( )	San Francisco ( )	Seaside ( )	West Covina ( )
National City ( )	Redlands ( )	San Gabriel ( )	Simi Valley ( )	Westminster ( )
Nevada City ( )	Redondo Beach ( )	San Jose ( )	South Gate ( )	
Oakland ( )	Redwood City ( )	San Leandro ( )	South San Francisco ( )	
Oceanside ( )	Rialto ( )	San Luis Obispo ( )	Stockton ( )	
Ontario ( )	Richmond ( )	San Mateo ( )	Sunnyvale ( )	

I started this section on the prevalence of gang-involved cities because the proliferation of street gangs across America is, to me, the most striking change of the past forty years. In the early 1960s, by my informal count, there were about sixty cities with street gangs, mostly in and around Southern California. By 1970, the number had increased to 100; by 1980, it had reached 180; and by 1992, when I gave up counting, over 750 cities had become gang involved.[2]

Since that time, the NYGC has been annually assessing the prevalence of gang-involved cities, towns, and county areas (even including Indian reservations), starting in 1996, which was the peak year in the NYGC's survey period. In that year, the NYGC estimated that there were 4,824 jurisdictions with active youth gangs. What an amazing number, even given the figures I noted above. In those jurisdictions, the NYGC estimated that there were 30,818 gangs and 846,428 active gang members. Gang proliferation exploded in the mid-1980s after a steady, but not shocking, rise in prior years. But 4,824 jurisdictions is indeed shocking. Fortunately, the number has declined somewhat since then, especially due to a decrease in smaller cities and rural areas; it is now closer to 3,000 jurisdictions.[3]

Now, let's go back to our three states and their 1996 gang city tests. In New York, there were twenty-six cities. Only Binghamton, Ithaca, New Rochelle, Poughkeepsie, Utica, and White Plains were gang free. Twenty New York cities had gang problems in 1996.

Next, look at the Iowa list. All fourteen cities were gang involved. Any Iowa city with more than 25,000 inhabitants had a street gang problem, defying the common image of the agricultural and rural heartland of America.

Finally, we look at California. I gave you a list of 141 towns and cities in our most populous state. All but nine of these had populations over 25,000, but the list probably includes a number of names you've never heard of. Even residents of California might have a hard time locating Antioch, Huron, Clovis, Milpitas, or Roseville, for example. Yet every one of these 141 cities was gang involved in 1996—you should have made 141 check marks! How deceiving the names can be: Palm Springs, Farmersville, Fountain Valley, Napa, Pleasant Hill, Paradise!

We should note, however, that smaller cities contribute small numbers to the overall gang picture. The biggest numbers, by far, are found in Los Angeles and Chicago, and more come from the communities immediately surrounding them. Outside of these areas, gangs are not generally common—the smaller the jurisdiction, the smaller the numbers. One can travel through, even stay in, most gang-involved cities, yet be unaware of the gangs. And if one does not visit areas with large youth concentrations, gangs can be almost invisible. Within the gang areas of a city, 10 or 15 percent of youth may be members; within most cities, only 1 or 2 percent of youth are gang members at any given time.[4]

Where gangs emerge is also related to time. There were street gangs in bigger cities starting in the 1920s and continuing thereafter until all really large cities had gangs by the early 1980s. Smaller cities started later and didn't explode on the scene until the late 1980s, continuing to the level of saturation seen in 1996 (roughly a quarter of the smallest cities and half of those in the 25,001-to-100,000 population range).

There are also some ethnic patterns of interest. Cities with predominantly black gang members tend to appear in the eastern half of the country—starting in eastern Texas and Oklahoma, and then everywhere north and east from there. Cities with predominantly Hispanic gang members are found more often in Texas and the southwestern states, as well as up and down California. Asian gangs are scattered about, but particularly in East Coast and West Coast cities where there are larger Asian communities. White gangs are also scattered about, but appear primarily in the midwestern states. It should be noted, however, that ethnicity is not a good distinguishing characteristic of street gangs. There are far more similarities than differences across black, Hispanic, Asian, and white street gangs.

These geographic distributions raise another interesting question: Has the proliferation of gangs into 4,000 jurisdictions resulted as gangs spread out from a few hubs like Los Angeles and Chicago, or has there been a spontaneous generation of indigenous groups in these many areas? In the mid-1980s, when crack cocaine became a national drug epidemic of sorts, it was widely reported that street gangs spread out in order to control crack distribution, or even general illegal drug distribution. Many police departments said so; the Federal Bureau of

Investigation (FBI) and Drug Enforcement Agency (DEA) said so; the media generally presented this view. Gangs and drugs became inseparable in the public's mind.

But independent research often fails to corroborate myth and conventional wisdom. Research in various cities (including Los Angeles, the earliest fabricator of the gangs/drug marketing stories) failed to support these reports.[5] While many gang members use drugs, most who sell them do so at a low level and mostly to their friends; they don't market them. While there are good examples of drug distribution gangs,[6] they are less common, and most gangs are not in the drug business. By and large, drug sales have been and still are largely in the hands of drug sellers who are only tangentially or not at all affiliated with street gangs.

A corollary to this is that research fails to support the common suggestion that gang proliferation across the country was due to drug franchising out of Los Angeles and Chicago. It is true that there has been gang member migration, but the emphasis should be on *members*; gangs per se do not migrate. However, research has shown that the primary reasons for gang member migration are personal and social—for example, the family move to search for employment or a better living environment. These are the same reasons many of us move from time to time. Migration specifically to spread and initiate drug sales or other criminal pursuits exists, but it is sporadic and not typical gang behavior. In a pivotal study, Maxson compared gang onset dates with dates of first gang migration.[7] She found that gangs start up in most cities largely prior to reported gang member migration from other cities and that the migration was more for social than for drug marketing reasons. Cities must accept responsibility for their gang developments; they cannot fairly blame them on outside forces.

I'll end this section on the proliferation of gangs with three special notes. The first is that the number of gangs (or gang cities) one claims to exist depends on how gangs are defined. For instance, the NYGC, whose work I have described in the enumeration of gang cities, deliberately avoided defining gangs for its police respondents around the country. Instead, it said a gang is "a group of youths or young adults in your jurisdiction that you or other responsible persons in your agency or community are willing to classify as a 'gang.' " [8] Basically, this is a non-definition. It includes taggers, satanic groups, "posses" and "crews," stoners, and terrorist groups, according to the police respondents. In addition, many respondents included "unsupervised youth groups," which obviously could include a wide variety of youthful friendship cliques and groups.

At my request, the NYGC then used a somewhat more restrictive definition of "gang" in a later sample of its respondents: "[a] group of youths or young adults in your jurisdiction whose involvement in illegal activities over months or years marks them in their own view and in the view of the community and police as different from most other youthful groups."[9] The result suggested that the original data overestimated the number of jurisdictions with gangs by 12 percent and the number of gangs by 26 percent. These are substantial overestimates. More restrictive definitions would have made the exaggeration even more serious.

The second special note is also, in part, definitional. Police estimates of gang prevalence are, of necessity, biased by their sources of information (gang members, victims, special interest groups). Police are not independent gang researchers. They tend to undercount smaller gangs, younger gang members not as yet arrested, female gang members, and minor crimes (which are far more common than major crimes). They tend, understandably, to overemphasize larger, enduring gangs; core gang members with serious crime records; and older gang members. Reliance on police gang reports can be very misleading (but, of course, most people *do* rely on those reports).

Finally, we consider a related point that is driven home by recent experience in Europe and in Central and South America. What academic scholars know about street gangs is highly related to their access to gang researchers, people actually engaged in studying gangs. Later in the book, I'll cover the issue of European street gangs in particular, but I want to note that in Europe, as in the United States, the number of gangs is unknown because those gangs have not been contacted by researchers. Gangs have proliferated in Europe far faster than gang researchers have. The same has been true in the United States. So what we know about where gangs are depends, along with definition, on who's counting. Our knowledge of gang prevalence is conditional on factors other than mere gang presence. We must beware of overstating our knowledge.

SPECIAL QUESTION: Most street gangs are in the largest cities. Why is this, and why do they emerge in small cities as well?

ENDNOTES

1. Details of the methods and results are reported in National Youth Gang Center, *1996 National Youth Gang Survey: Summary* (Washington, D.C.: U.S. Department of Justice, Office of Juvenile Justice and Delinquency Prevention, July 1999).

2. These cities are shown in four consecutive maps in Chapter 4 of my book *The American Street Gang: Its Nature, Prevalence, and Control* (Oxford, England: Oxford University Press, 1995).

3. Data for the period from 1996 to 2002 are reported in Arlen Egley, Jr., James C. Howell, and Celine K. Major, "Recent Patterns of Gang Problems in the United States," in *American Youth Gangs at the Millennium*, edited by Finn-Aage Esbensen, Stephen G. Tibbets, and Larry Gaines (Long Grove, Ill: Waveland Press, 2004). The likely reasons for the proliferation of street gangs are many and controversial. The reader may wish to read the discussion in Chapter 7 of my book *The American Street Gang* (1995).

4. Relevant data for 12- to 16-year-olds are reported in Howard N. Snyder and Melissa Sickmund, *Juvenile Offenders and Victims: 1999 National Report* (Washington, D.C.: U.S. Department of Justice, Office of Juvenile Justice and Delinquency Prevention, 1999).

5. See references to Decker (2001), Maxson (1995), and Klein and Maxson (1994).

6. See references to Padilla (1992), McGarrell and Chermak (2003), and Valdez and Sifanek (2004).

7. See Maxson (1993, 1998) for the drug and migration connections.

8. National Youth Gang Center (1999).

9. Klein and Maxson (2006), Introduction.

| **STREET GANGS AND OTHER GROUPS**

T he definitional issue just covered is complex: The boundaries between gang and non-gang can be ambiguous or even arbitrary. Let's try our hand at labeling some youth groups. Which of the following are street gangs?

Group A: A group of seven Asian teenagers drove up to a small private dance club and confronted the club's unofficial bouncer. There was a small melée, during which a chair was thrown and several blows were struck. At the end, a gun was fired toward the club, but the bullet went through the window of a neighboring video store, killing the owner. The teenagers were described by the police as a clique that had recently broken off from a larger "tagger crew." The clique members clearly had been cruising around looking for trouble— they may have been involved in a store burglary the hour before the shooting incident—but were quite unknown to the police for anything but minor offenses. Was group A a street gang?

Group B: A group of four boys was involved in a stabbing of a fifth at a local beach. Under special state anti-gang legislation, the four assailants were prosecuted as a criminal street gang, being labeled a "bully gang" by the prosecution. They comprised a suburban clique adopting 1950s-style haircuts and clothing to mark them as a special group. They manifested no meaningful street life and had little prior criminal involvement. Was group B, the bully gang, a street gang?

Group C: An off-duty sheriff's deputy spotted several youths putting up their graffiti on a wall. When they failed to obey his command to cease and resisted arrest, he fired his gun in their direction. The deputy was charged with ADW (assault with a deadly weapon). The defense claimed that his action was a legitimate response to the criminal acts of a street gang. Was he correct that group C was a street gang?

Group D: A police patrol was dispatched to the "old town" section of a city on a report that a group of skinheads had gathered in this tourist area and was loitering and disturbing the peace by wandering the streets, shouting slogans, and upsetting tourists and businesses in the area. Upon their arrival, the police confronted the group, but received only polite responses—"Good evening, officers," "Isn't it a lovely evening for a walk?" and so on. Were the police confronting a street gang in group D?

Group E: In reaction to an anonymous tip, the FBI raided a small club and detained the adult members of a group gathered there. A search of the facility yielded a cache of automatic weapons, materials for making explosives, and literature proclaiming a war against the U.S. government, including the FBI and a number of prominent politicians. Evidence also indicated that the club's finances came from a series of burglaries and the sale of narcotics. Was group E a street gang?

Group F: Wire taps on telephone conversations from a maximum security prison captured conversations between members of Nuestra Familia, a large Latino group of convicts inside the prison, and other members of the group on the outside. The core of the conversations had to do with a contract "hit" on a rival who had to be "dealt with." The convicts were charged with solicitation and conspiracy to commit murder: Were they part of a street gang?

Group G: A member of a group calling itself the Miranda Car Club attempts to steal a car from a parking area. He is interrupted by two Hispanic males who shoot him twice as he tries to escape. Then three additional Hispanic males attack him; he is shot again, resulting in permanent paralysis. The victim's car club is not classified by the city police department as a gang, but the victim claims that the attack was a targeted "hit" by the assailants, members of a rival gang. Was the rival group, group G, a street gang?

Group H: The Del Vikings were an acknowledged and self-admitted younger street gang, a clique associated with a larger traditional gang known as the Gladiators. The Del Vikings were, on average, about thirteen years old. A small number of their girlfriends, sisters, and cousins often hung around on the street with the boys, calling themselves the Viqueens. They met as a group at the same time as did the boys, but their delinquent activity was considerably lower than that of the boys. Should group H, the Viqueens, be classed as a street gang?

I'll return to these cases in a few pages. But first, let me illustrate the importance of distinguishing gangs from other youth groups. Several decades ago, engaging in "gang activity" was illegal in California until a judge ruled the law unconstitutional due to the vagueness of the term. He did so after two rookie police officers spotted a group of fifteen youths gathered together in an area of town known to include street gangs. The officers detained all fifteen, called for backup, and had these "gang members" taken to Juvenile Hall and held for trial for engaging in gang activity. The trial revealed that the officers had no training in recognizing gang members and had in fact arrested fifteen local kids who had just exited from a Saturday afternoon movie matinee.

The problem with distinguishing street gangs from other youth groups is that street gangs are usually unsponsored, unsupervised, and rather informal groups. They have no constitutions and by-laws, membership rosters, required dues, written rules of conduct, and position descriptions. How then can they be defined so that we can distinguish between groups that are gangs and groups that are not?

The question sounds simple, yet gang scholars have wrestled with it for the past eighty years, without achieving consensus. One problem has been that each scholar attempting a definition has been limited to the few gangs he or she has studied. Another problem has been the question of whether or not illegal behavior is intrinsic to the nature of street gangs. A third problem has been the confusion between factors that define and distinguish gangs from other groups and factors that are commonly used to describe gangs, factors such as size, structure, special clothing, special signs and language, leadership, and so on. Let's look briefly at perhaps the most widely cited gang definitions as they have evolved over time:

- "The gang is an interstitial group originally formed spontaneously, and then integrated through conflict. It is characterized by the following types of behavior: meeting face to face, milling, movement through space as a unit, conflict, and planning. The result of this collective behavior is the development of tradition, unreflective internal structure, esprit de corps, solidarity, morale, group awareness, and attachment to a local territory." (Thrasher 1927, 48)

- "For our purposes, we shall use the term *gang* to refer to any denotable adolescent group of youngsters who (a) are generally perceived as a distinct aggregation by others in their neighborhood, (b) recognize themselves as a denotable group (almost invariably with a group name) and (c) have been involved in a sufficient number of delinquent incidents to call forth a consistent negative response from neighborhood residents and/or enforcement agencies." (Klein 1971, 13)

- "A youth gang is a self-formed association of peers, bound together by mutual interests, with identifiable leadership, well-developed lines of authority, and other organizational features, who act in concert to achieve a specific purpose or purposes which generally include the conduct of illegal activity and control over a particular territory, facility, or type of enterprise." (Miller 1980, 121)

- "Gangs are groups whose members meet together with some regularity, over time, on the basis of group-defined criteria of membership and group-defined organizational characteristics; that is, gangs are non-adult sponsored, self-determining groups that demonstrate continuity over time." (Short 1996, 5)

- ". . . any ongoing organization, association, or group of three or more persons, whether formal or informal, having as one of its primary activities the commission of one or more of the criminal acts enumerated in paragraphs (1) to (8), inclusive, of subdivision (E), which has a common name or common identifying sign or symbol, whose members individually or collectively engage in or have engaged in a pattern of criminal gang activity." (California Penal Code, sec. 186.22)

- "A group of youths or young adults in your jurisdiction that you or other responsible persons in your agency or community are willing to identify or classify as a 'gang.'" (NYGC, 1999)

There is a rough progression to these definitional attempts, as they become less specific as to the descriptive characteristics of gangs, but still a clear common core does not emerge. The NYGC definition has become so non-specific that it is really a non-definition: A gang is whatever you think it is. As I noted earlier, this is not helpful.

Finally—and fortunately—I think we have come to a significant point of possible agreement on a broadly applicable definition of street gangs. It resulted from intense discussions among working groups of American and European gang researchers over a six-year period as part of what has come to be known as The Eurogang Program.[1] This consensus Eurogang definition—the basis for all my discussion in this book—reads as follows:

The Eurogang Consensus Nominal Definition of Street Gangs
"A Street Gang Is Any Durable, Street-Oriented Youth Group Whose Own Identity Includes Involvement in Illegal Activity."

Point 1: "durable" is a bit ambiguous, but at least several months can be used as a guideline. Many gang-like groups come together and dissipate within a few months. The durability refers to the *group*, which continues despite turnover of members.

Point 2: "street-oriented" implies spending a lot of group time outside home, work, and school—often on streets, in malls, in parks, in cars, and so on.

Point 3: "youth" can be ambiguous. Most street gangs are more adolescent than adult, but some include members in their twenties and even thirties. Most have average ages in adolescence or early twenties.

Point 4: "illegal" generally means delinquent or criminal, not just bothersome.

Point 5: "identity" refers to the group, not the individual self-image.

This definition accomplishes several things. First, it is a minimalist statement that includes only the necessary and sufficient definers of street gangs—durability, street orientation, youthfulness, group status (not just a collection of individuals), and identity based in part on illegal activity. Second, it excludes all the gang *descriptors* of prior definitions, which can then be used to describe variations in gang characteristics (for example, size, ethnicity, names, use of signs or symbols, levels of violence). Third, it effectively omits other crime groups such as prison gangs, motorcycle gangs, terrorist groups, and adult criminal enterprises. Fourth, it distinguishes street gangs from the far more numerous formal as well as informal youth groups to which many of us belonged. With this definition, street gangs are relatively distinguishable from most other groups and can therefore be studied and understood as a fairly distinct phenomenon.

Now let's go back to the eight group descriptions and make some judgment calls about their gang status. Group A, the new spin-off clique that got itself into the same serious trouble, most probably could fit under our definition, but it's a close call.

Group B, the "bully gang," should not be included: It has low street orientation and a low level of illegal identity. The prosecutors merely called the four boys a gang in order to fit them within special anti-gang legislation. The judge in the case, after hearing the arguments, threw out the gang allegations.

Group C seemed to be a "tagger crew," one of many such groups who specialize in making their mark via special graffiti, but otherwise fail the illegal identity test.

Group D, the skinheads who effectively disarmed the police confrontation with their polite veneer, do fit under our definition. As we will see later, they constitute one example of a category called specialty gangs.

Group E, probably a terrorist gang, does not fit. It fails the youth test and the street-orientation test. Similarly, Group F fails the same tests. Nuestra Familia is a notorious prison gang. While there are instances of documented relationships between prison gangs and street gangs, they are generally of a very different character.[2]

Group G is a tougher call because we have so little information. Car clubs are not street gangs, but the victim's claim of a "hit" by a rival gang at least raises the question. Still, it is far better to avoid the label "gang" in the absence of good evidence because this can stigmatize a group.

Group H, the Viqueens, is an auxiliary to the Del Vikings street gang. The fact that it is a female group in no way precludes gang status. There are autonomous girl gangs (although they are uncommon), and there are many girl gangs that affiliate, like the Viqueens, with male gangs. In many instances, girls are involved in integrated or mixed-gender gangs. Gender is a descriptor, not a definition.

So, out of a list of eight candidate groups, we probably have three that can be labeled street gangs and five that might be confused with street gangs. Definitions don't settle the issue; they provide guidelines for judgment calls. Much of my work as an expert witness in court cases involves helping the jury to decide whether or not the defendant is a member of a street gang and therefore subject to the additional penalties provided under anti-gang legislation. It's a judgment that makes a difference to both the prosecution and the defense.

I can add to this exercise the good news that this consensus definition of gangs has now been applied by an increasing number of researchers to groups in the United States and in Europe, with considerable success. It is proving to be a remedy to the stereotyping of street gangs as large, hierarchical, violent groups in the West Side Story mold, and it is encouraging greater attention to gang comparisons across many settings.

But our definitional concerns do not end here. Another commonly raised issue is, What is gang-related crime? Two approaches to the question have been taken, both dictated by police concerns for documenting how much street gang crime takes place. Let's consider two examples.

- Pedro Lupino (aka "Petey-Dog"), a member of the Ladino Hills gang, pulled a gun on two younger boys in his local park, demanding their money. He warned them that if they told the police about the robbery, he would shoot them.
- Peter Wolff (aka "Lil Congo"), a member of the 10th Street Crips, confronted two members of the rival Two-Four Bloods who were spraying the walls in his local park with "Crip Killer" signs. He pulled a gun on them, took their money, and warned them that if they were seen in his territory again, he or his homies would shoot them.

Are these two incidents examples of gang-related crime? Unfortunately, the answer depends on which police jurisdiction is involved. In some jurisdictions, Petey-Dog's armed robbery and threat comprise an individually motivated crime with no gang implications. It will not be recorded as a gang crime and will not be prosecuted as a gang crime with the possible additional punishment that accompanies a "gang allegation." But Lil Congo's robbery and threat will be recorded and presented as a gang-related crime.

In other jurisdictions, both events will be treated as gang crimes. The difference is definitional. "Gang-related" can mean, very broadly, any crime in which a gang member is involved; then both of our incidents fit. But if gang-related is defined as "gang-motivated," as carried out *because* of gang issues, then only Lil Congo's crime is gang-related— he was defending his gang's territory against an incursion by rival gang members. Petey-Dog's crime could just as easily have been committed by me—or you—neither of us having any motive other than pure greed.

Does it make a difference? Yes, in two ways. First, research using Chicago and Los Angeles cases revealed that the gang-motivated crimes were only half as common as crimes involving gang members, regardless of gang motive. The choice of definition, not the acts, determines the level of gang-related crime reported by the police. When the Chicago "motive" definition was applied to the reported Los Angeles "member"-defined homicides, the gang homicide rate for Los Angeles was cut in half.[3] There are political implications no matter which approach is taken. If you want to increase resources to combat gang crime, count the crimes using the "member" definition because it will maximize the size of the problem. On the other hand, if you want to minimize the gang crime problem and claim it is under control, use the "motive" definition, which greatly restricts the numbers of gang offenses. Second, if the "motive" definition is used, then prosecutors can push for additional punishments—more years in prison—in only half as many cases. This is not what prosecutors want.

Let's add one more complication, one that arose principally after the early 1980s and the explosion of crack cocaine sales across the country. An increasing number of homicides were associated with narcotic sales, and gangs were reputedly associated with some or many of these (depending on which research and police reports are read). Many police reporting systems are set up to designate a homicide as gang related (however defined) or narcotics related, but not both. All the discussion above flies out the window if a homicide committed by or against a gang member is recorded as narcotics related. At one point, the gang unit supervisor in Philadelphia admitted to me that a precipitous decline in reported gang-related homicides had been accomplished by listing a lot of them as narcotics related instead. In Chicago, by way of contrast, despite that city's high level of connections between gangs and narcotics sales, almost all such homicides are recorded as gang related.

Gang statistics aren't worthless—far from it—but they certainly can be ambiguous. What we have seen in Sections 1 and 2 of this book is that the number of gangs documented across the country can vary substantially depending on how gangs are defined. The amount of gang crime reported across the country similarly depends on how such crimes are defined. It is not enough to count on the NYGC or the FBI or our local authorities to be accurate. They can offer only approximations, and these will differ depending on who is doing the reporting. There are no nationally accepted and implemented standards for assessing the level of street gang prevalence or gang crime. One needs to understand the definitions employed.[4]

SPECIAL QUESTION: Are five gang "definers" really enough, or is there something to be gained by adding a few "descriptors" to the list?

ENDNOTES

1. The issues and processes are fully spelled out in two books in the list of Selected Supplemental Readings at the end of this book, Klein et al. (2001) and Klein and Maxson (2006).

2. A useful discussion of prison gang issues can be found in a special issue of *The Corrections Management Quarterly* (2001, 5, no. 1).

3. See Maxson and Klein (1990, 1996).

4. One can go from the ambiguous to the ridiculous. In June 2004, the Los Angeles Regional Gang Information Network (LARGIN), open "to all law enforcement entities in the Los Angeles County that are investigating criminal gang activity," promulgated a set of criteria for determining what is a gang-related crime. In the following statement, I emphasize in particular LARGIN's statement that "[o]*ne* or more of the following gang related criteria shall be used to justify that a crime is gang related." One, it seems, is enough.

> Any crime can constitute a gang related crime when the suspect or the victim is an active or affiliate gang member; or when circumstances indicate that the crime is consistent with gang activity. Determining if a crime is gang related is subjective in nature and is a result of the totality of the circumstances. Classification cannot be accomplished accurately without a high degree of gang expertise or validation through the Cal Gang system. One or more of the following gang related criteria shall be used to justify that a crime is gang related.

> The suspect or victim is a known gang member previously entered into the Cal Gang system.

> The suspect or victim is a known gang member or affiliate.

> The suspect or victim has a gang tattoo.

> The suspect or victim has a gang moniker.

> A statement indicating gang involvement was made.

> The suspect or victim was "dressed down" or wearing gang colors or clothing.

> The suspect or victim was demonstrating gang behavior. (Using gang hand signs)

> Multiple suspects and gang modus operandi were involved.

> The location of the crime was within identified gang boundaries or at a known gang location.

> Similar reports were made where the suspects were identified as gang members.

> The type and/or modus operandi of the crime are inherently gang related.

> A reliable informant identifies a crime as gang related.

> An informant of previously untested reliability identifies a crime as gang related and it is corroborated by other independent information.

All of the above warnings, you can be sure, will apply as well to the issue of who is and is not a street gang member, and not just because of the ambiguities in defining what a gang is. It goes well beyond that shaky beginning because there are issues of not only who *is* a gang member, but also how much of a gang member and when? For instance, longitudinal gang studies in several cities suggest that average time in a gang is only around one year. I'll illustrate these issues with some criminal cases that actually went to court, but first let me cite three cautions.

The first caution is that understanding gang versus non-gang youth requires the proper setting. It makes little sense to compare youth from an affluent area to those from an inner-city area. Whether the inner-city kids are gang or not gang, they'll be very different from the more privileged youth. We need to compare gang and non-gang kids *from the same neighborhood*, where context is controlled—the same for each. The second caution is that, even in the most gang-involved neighborhoods, most kids don't join gangs. The 10 or 15 percent of those who do join are different from those who don't, but not with respect to local levels of poverty, social resources, racism, job opportunities, and so on. The third caution is simply this: Since most kids are not gang members, we must be careful not to judge by appearances alone. Recall from Section 2 the fifteen "gang members" who were arrested by two rookie officers, only to emerge as local youngsters leaving a movie theater. Or recall group D, the skinhead gang members who interacted so courteously with police officers, as if they were the most innocent of innocents.

When I started out in gang research, I, too, was vulnerable to misidentifying gang and non-gang members. Early on, I was sitting in the small bleachers of a local park, in the midst of eight or nine adolescents, watching a pick-up football game on the field. The play was very rough, and rules were disregarded or made up as the need arose. My fellow onlookers were vociferous in their support of the action before us. I was informed an hour later by a gang worker that the game participants were local school kids and that I had been sitting in the midst of the core members of the local street gang. I had no idea, but in my naïveté I would have guessed just the opposite.

Not long thereafter, I was driving home in the dusk after observing a gang meeting in another area. I observed a group of young blacks gathered outside my local movie theater in my all-white suburban neighborhood. I pulled over to watch the gang in action—after all, I was a newly minted gang researcher—only to observe two church vans pull up and load the youth volunteers in for their ride home. I was very annoyed at myself.

And, finally, there was the time I was driving my shamefully rusted-out car to an evening gang meeting and spotted several of the members I had observed in boisterous street corner behavior earlier in the day. I pulled over, asked if they were going to the meeting (they were), and gave them a ride. Over the next ten minutes, I was treated to the most courteous, middle-class repertory of polite conversation anyone could expect from the shiniest young men in town. These were gang members, normally spouting f--- this and m----- f--- ing that with every opening of their mouths, giving me their other side. I had one repertoire; they had two. I could fit in only one setting; they could fit in two. They were my version of the polite skinheads of group D. Labeling someone a gang member takes more than a simple observation.

Given the widespread stereotypes of gangs and gang members, the tendency of the media to emphasize the worst aspects of both, and the fact that most youths are not gang members, even in the most gang-involved communities, we can fairly assume that the general public—and many readers of this book—would overidentify young people as gang members. These incorrect labels of "gang member" are called false positives.

History suggests that many police officers experience false positives as well; they see more gang members than really exist. It is still the case that if you spot a young male with baggy pants, a white t-shirt, and a shaved head hanging around a park, he is probably not a gang member. If you see a young male with tattoos and an earring on the schoolyard, he is probably not a gang member. If you hear such a youth using foul language and disturbing other people around him on the street corner, he is probably not a gang member. Of course, in each case he may turn out to be gang affiliated, but the odds are against it.

The toughest test comes when we view purported gang members in criminal court. There, a particular crime may sound gang related. The police witness may well claim that the defendant is a gang member. And the prosecutor will often try to prove to the jury that the defendant is a gang member in hopes of getting a more serious sentence upon his conviction. (The laws in many states punish gang members more severely than non-gang members for identical criminal offenses.)

The examples that follow are taken from actual court cases in which I have been involved as a consultant or as an expert witness. In each case, we find ambiguities or certainties as to whether the defendant *is* a street gang member, or how much of a member he or she is, at what level, and for how long.

1. *Two Questionable Gang Members:* Our first defendant is a fifteen-year-old boy for whom no indications were presented by the prosecutor that he was a gang member—no tattoos, no gang admissions, no prior arrests, no listing in the police gang files, and so on. He was involved in a robbery with two others, one of whom was an older, hardened gang member who bullied and threatened the fifteen-year-old. The young defendant had strong musical skills. He had caring, although separated, parents. He was bright, used no alcohol or drugs, and had a steady girlfriend. Because he was involved in a "gang-connected" crime, the prosecution charged him as a gang member. Was he a gang member?

The second defendant is a young woman in her senior year at a small church-related college in the East. While visiting her parents—united, both civil servants in a city on the West Coast—she was asked by her parents to drive out to a suburb to pick up and deliver her twin brother, a hardcore gang member wanted on a murder warrant. She herself had no prior indications of gang involvement. She picked up her brother, who was accompanied by two of his friends. On the way back to surrender, the brother asked her to stop near a bar. While she waited around the corner, they entered the bar, assaulted and shot several employees, and robbed the safe. They returned to the car and told the defendant to drive toward town. A pursuit followed with police cars and helicopters, but she was forced by the passengers in the car to continue driving until they finally told her to pull over. They ran off, unsuccessfully, while she remained in the driver's seat following the instructions from the police. She was charged with fleeing the scene of a crime, with aiding and abetting the armed robbery, and with being a gang member by virtue of her association with her hardcore brother. Was she a gang member?

2. *Various Levels of Gang Membership:* Our first defendant in this category was charged with being a gang member. He was developmentally limited and spent a good deal of time hanging around with older peers. During an arrest for loitering with two of his companions, he was found to be drunk. He admitted to being a member of their gang, but a day later denied membership and had no memory of the admission. There were no other mentions of him in the arrest or probation reports of his companions. To what level of membership should he be assigned?

The next defendant held up a female driver, demanding her money. He was charged with armed robbery with intent to further the goals of his small, neighborhood gang. Testimony revealed that he was being extorted by members of a far larger and violent gang. On a day he couldn't pay up, he was thrown through a store window, cutting him extensively. The following week, he held up the female victim with a BB gun to get some money for the extortion payoff. She had no money, but offered the keys to her car. He declined, saying he just needed some money, and walked away. How "ganged up" was he? Was his act in furtherance of his gang's goals?

The third defendant in this category is a thirteen-year-old boy who was charged with ADW (assault with a deadly weapon). He was described as the victim of birth trauma, with diagnoses of Attention Deficit Hyperactivity Disorder, possible Post-Traumatic Stress Disorder, and Tourette's syndrome. His mother was a longtime drug abuser, now paraplegic, while his father had an extensive history of antisocial behavior. His older brother was killed in a gang confrontation. The boy had been on medications, including Ritalin, but balancing them had proven difficult. In addition, this youngster had several different gang affiliations, starting at age eleven. His record included threats of assault against his grandparents with a poker and a razor. He bragged about his gang affiliations and various sexual exploits and exhibited extensive knowledge of gang culture and practices. At age thirteen, was this merely a young "wannabe" on the make or a young gang psychopath?

3. *The Gang Associate:* This term is often used in court when gang membership cannot be clearly established. Such was the case in a highly publicized cop-killer incident. Two young men were sitting in a car in a motel parking lot. The driver was a heavy-duty gang member in possession of a load of methamphetamines. A police officer noticed that the two young males in the car looked out of place and that the car had no plates. He radioed for backup and then approached the car. The driver fired shots at him, but was killed by return fire. The passenger—our defendant—panicked and opened fire at the approach of a second officer, killing him. The defendant was charged with murder as a gang member. He had Attention Deficit Hyperactivity Disorder, was a school dropout and a loner, and was called dumb over and over by his parents. He joined a party crew and a tagger crew, but had no recorded gang affiliations and only one minor misdemeanor charge on his record. Should he have been charged as a gang member or as a gang associate? The penal code does not have a section on or definition of a "gang associate."

4. *Changing Levels of Gang Membership:* Levels of gang membership do not remain stable. At age fourteen, our next defendant was a peripheral gang member involved in a few minor scrapes. His parents moved him to live with his grandmother in a new town to

escape the gang environment. However, his grandmother began losing control over him, his school performance faltered, his attitude hardened, and he joined a local street gang in the new town. At age seventeen, he was charged as an accomplice to murder, with additional gang allegations. Is there any problem with this gang charge? The judge said no.

Another defendant had a strong mother, holding down two jobs. She, too, moved her boy out of a high-crime area. In his new setting, he played high school soccer, basketball, and football. He maintained a 2.8 grade point average. He was helped along by a teacher who became his mentor, and in turn he served as a tutor to other students. He also participated regularly in church activities. At age sixteen, he was riding in a car with friends who committed a drive-by shooting, and he pled guilty to second-degree assault, a misdemeanor. He was allowed to complete high school before serving a six-month sentence.

Then, in a clear trajectory out of trouble, he moved out of state to attend a community college, playing on the football team and maintaining a C grade point average. He had good reports on his progress, plans to move on to a four-year college, and no signs of gang affiliation or any other trouble. One evening, he was asked for a ride by several friends who, it turned out, were gang members. Once again, there was a drive-by shooting in which the victim died and two others were wounded. The defendant testified that he was unaware of the guns or any intention of a shooting. Here is a young man who was moving away from trouble and preparing satisfactorily for an adult life, but who then made a dumb and costly mistake, perhaps allowing himself to be used by others. Should he be charged, still, as a gang member? My testimony said no.

5. *The Reformed Gang Member:* A very young Cambodian-American boy from a dysfunctional family situation claimed membership in a local

Asian gang on the West Cost, but then was moved to the East where there was no Cambodian community and where he exhibited no known indications of gang affiliation. Still affected by the family situation, he moved to the Northwest to live with his older brother, who, unfortunately, was a strong role model of the wrong kind. At age fifteen, he was taken by his brother and another older boy to rob a female store owner. In the confrontation, the brother shot and killed the woman. In order to get the maximum sentence, the prosecutor charged the fifteen-year-old with gang-related murder and asked that he be tried as an adult. It had been some years since the boy had shown any documented gang affiliations. Should he have been handled as a juvenile and sent for six years to a rehabilitative juvenile correctional center, or should he have been waived to adult court, where he could be sentenced to twenty-five years or more in prison? The judge denied the gang charge, and the boy was handled as a juvenile.

Our last defendant is an ex-gang member, a two-striker (two felony convictions) who is now fifty years old. He had been working as a volunteer in a gang reduction program. One evening, he received a call from a gang member who had been told he had to go out on a "hit," because he had a gun, but he was afraid to go. Our defendant agreed to retrieve the gun to give the member an excuse not to get involved, but to do so, he took his girlfriend's car without her permission. She called the police. When he returned with the car and the gun, he found the police waiting for him. He was arrested for possession of a firearm—a third strike. The girlfriend declined to press charges, and the boy's family corroborated the story of the gun. Nonetheless, under the theory of "once a gang member, always a gang member," the district attorney decided to push the third-strike charge in order to put the defendant away for twenty-five years to life. Is there a legitimate gang charge here? In my view, no, and that's what I advised his attorney.

When one can be said to have joined a street gang, what level of membership one exhibits and at what times, and when one leaves a gang are all judgment calls, as many of the above cases illustrate. Different people will offer different judgments based on knowledge, stereotype, and the purpose of the judgment. This is possible because street gangs are informal groups, not formal organizations where membership status needs to be established. Further, how we estimate the numbers of gangs or the sizes of gangs depends heavily on how we define them and how selectively we are exposed to them.

Across 29 recent reports assessing the proportion of gang members in the youth population, the estimates range from a low of 2 percent to a high of 37 percent.[1] This wide range reflects the different locations and samples used, as well as differences in definition. The best guess, for a national estimate, would be in the neighborhood of 5 percent. Estimates for female gang members in the youth population range from 0 to 29 percent, depending on the same factors. Something well below 5 percent would be the best guess for female gang membership overall, while the proportion of all gang members who are female is often found to be 15 percent or more. However defined and measured, gang youth like those portrayed in these court cases are in large supply, even though they comprise a small proportion of all youth.

What brings youth to the gang is less clear. Certainly at the societal level, we can blame racism, poverty, and unemployment. At other levels—individual, family, peer, school, and neighborhood—recent compilations of the available research tell us that most youth, most group members, and most delinquent kids do not become gang members.[2] The last point—that most delinquents do not become gang members—is pivotal. It suggests that many of the variables used to predict delinquency, and there are scores of such variables, probably won't help us to predict which kids will join gangs. A recent summary of what are called "risk factors" for gang joining, taken from twenty comprehensive studies over the past fifteen years (Klein and Maxson 2006, chap. 4), pinpoints only the following categories of variables as making gang joining more likely:

- Negative life events (e.g., death in the family, physical abuse)
- Non-delinquent problem behavior (e.g., impulsiveness, fighting, excessive drinking)
- Delinquent beliefs (e.g., OK to steal small things, might makes right)
- Low parental supervision (e.g., low monitoring of friends, low general supervision)
- Low academic achievement (e.g., low commitment to school, poor grades)
- Characteristics of the peer network (e.g., delinquent friends, unsupervised groups)
- Affective dimensions of the peer network (e.g., loyalty to group, sense of marginality)

Let's face it: This is a pitifully meager list of risk factors for gang joining, yet these are the only constructs that consistently emerge from the twenty studies reviewed. Knowing these is better than nothing; knowing that most things people *might* nominate as risk factors don't make the grade is very important. Obviously, we have a very long way to go before we can effectively predict who will become gang members. The best prediction for any one individual, male or female, of any ethnicity is that he or she won't join a gang.

SPECIAL QUESTION: Should being a gang member make a difference when determining the punishment for criminal behavior?

ENDNOTES

1. See Chapter 1 in Klein and Maxson (2006) for these and other prevalence estimates.

2. The parallel to at least one other situation is quite striking. Consider this description of the enrollment of "boy soldiers" throughout the world (Brett and Specht 2004, 3–4):

> It is indeed true that most child soldiers come from impoverished circumstances, and not only in Africa. However, many poor children do not become child soldiers. Thus it is clear that although poverty may create a general vulnerability to military recruitment, it cannot be the only factor.
>
> Such general environmental factors set the context without which involvement is highly unlikely to happen. There is a second level of factors, however, relating to the individual's personal history, which predisposes certain young people to join the army or the conflict, while others who share the same general environment do not. Indeed the precise combination of factors that lead in each individual case to this decision is unique. Even then it is not decisive. In each individual story there is a third level: there is a trigger for the specific decision to join up. What is it that tips the balance from thinking about it to taking the decision and acting on it? Some young people think about joining for years before actually doing so. Obviously many who do not join also think about the possibility, but the particular combination of factors does not occur, or there are countervailing ones. By contrast, some have not considered it at all until their world disintegrates and they see no other option. Many of the same factors that set the scene or are part of the more specific situation of the young person are often the ones that crystallize into a particular moment of decision.

SECTION 4 | STREET GANG CRIMES DEFINED

For the most part, street gang members commit a wide variety of illegal offenses—underage drinking and sex, vandalism (including graffiti), drug use, drug selling, petty theft, assault, burglary, robbery, auto theft, and so on. The greater part of this crime is minor—property damage, theft, and the like—while truly serious offenses, such as robbery, assault, and murder, are relatively uncommon. Nonetheless, it is these more serious offenses that capture media attention, create fear in some communities, and end up receiving the more concentrated attention of the police and the courts. Thus, it is these more serious offenses that will concern us in Section 4.

We have to make an important distinction here between crimes that gang members might commit whether they are members or not (all the crimes that you and I commit, I presume, are not a function of our gang membership) and crimes that are "gang related." Here's where again we get into the definitional morass discussed at the end of Section 2. What is a gang-related crime? I'm going to offer a number of examples, but first let's look at several meanings of "gang related."

THREE DEFINITIONS OF GANG-RELATED CRIME

The first two definitions have traditionally been used by police departments, each associated with either Los Angeles or Chicago, the largest contributors to the nation's gang problem. The Los Angeles definition, which we label "member-defined" gang crime, states that any crime is gang related if a gang member is involved on either the offender or the victim side. The Chicago definition is said to be "motive defined" and labels as gang related any crime committed as a result of a gang purpose. Examples could include retaliation, witness intimidation, graffiti placement or removal, drive-by shootings, drug trafficking for profit sharing in the gang, and offenses used as initiation into the gang.

Motive-defined crime is harder to establish than member-defined crime, since it involves inferences about the offender's intent. Research undertaken with my colleague Cheryl Maxson (Maxson and Klein 1990, 1996) applied both definitions to hundreds of gang and non-gang homicides in the Los Angeles region. We found that the use of the member definition yielded approximately twice as many "gang-related" homicides as did the motive definition. As noted earlier, politicians and police agencies seeking funds to combat gang violence would do well to employ the member definition; those wishing to minimize the problem for public relations purposes would benefit from the motive definition. They represent different "realities" of gang violence. However, our research analysis also revealed that the member-defined and motive-defined homicides did not differ substantially in their character—the offenders looked the same, the victims looked the same, and the physical settings and crime characteristics looked the same. The differences are definitional, but not substantive.

The third definition, written into the penal codes of many states, takes the motive definition to its extreme. A crime is "gang related" if it was deliberately committed in the furtherance of gang goals (i.e., a group motive, not an individual one) or at the direction of the gang. For instance, if I shoot someone to enhance *my* reputation in the gang, this is motive defined. But if I do it to enhance the *gang's* reputation, then this is furtherance of gang goals. In states using this furtherance definition in court, the convicted offender can have many years added to his prison sentence. Prosecutors, you can well understand, often employ this sentence-enhancing definition zealously. Defense attorneys have fought against it with equal vigor.

We need some examples to illustrate how these three definitions might apply in real life. Once again, I turn to actual court cases where all this is played out.

1. *Member-Defined Gang Crimes:* Our first case in this category is notorious. Following the vicious police beating of motorist Rodney King, a black man, an all-white suburban jury found the police innocent of all charges. This verdict initiated one of the worst urban riots in U.S. history, as fire, looting, and mayhem swept through central and south Los Angeles. Just as King's beating was captured on television and broadcast throughout the world, so was the horrible beating of a white truck driver by young blacks at the epicenter of the riots, while the police retreated to their station house and their chief kept a prior speaking engagement in a nearby town. The truck driver's principal assailant was a known member of a large traditional gang, showing off his brutal prowess to the television cameras in the news helicopters overhead. This was a riot-motivated assault, not a gang-motivated one,

but it was defined as gang related by virtue of the offender's gang membership.

The second case involves the street robbery of a forty-eight-year-old, Mandarin-speaking Chinese man. There was no gun involved, and only $40 was taken. The offender was caught soon thereafter and found to be an inactive or former gang member (his membership being documented one and a half years earlier). The prosecutor pursued a charge that the robbery was in furtherance of gang goals, but could offer no evidence to support this gang-related definition. The member definition fits, but only if one accepts an indication of membership that is a year and a half old. Do you think this was a gang-related crime or merely an ordinary street robbery?

Our third case is a bit more complex. During a bank robbery a hundred miles away from their home territory, the defendant and three co-defendants shot and killed a female bank customer. Evidence shows that this was an impulsive, unplanned event and that the money was divided up among the robbers. Although four gang members were involved, the distance from their turf and the division of the spoils did not support a charge that the robbery was done in furtherance of gang goals. Certainly, the shooting of a bank customer could not reasonably be considered gang motivated. Therefore, the event is gang related only because the robbers were gang members.

In our fourth member-related case, a fringe member of a gang assaulted his former girlfriend. The prosecution claimed the gang furtherance goal, but clearly this was a domestic dispute. Domestic disputes usually are excluded by the police from even the member definition. Would you accept this as a member-defined gang-related crime or as a non-gang domestic assault? Let's expand on this question with a few more ambiguous cases.

2. *Questionable Member-Defined Gang Crimes:* A defendant was not a gang member, but from his neighborhood he knew a lot about gangs. He had been shot at, so he carried a gun. On this occasion, he was harassed and threatened by members of a small local gang. Feeling threatened, he fired his gun and was charged with ADW (assault with a deadly weapon). He claimed self-defense. Was this a gang-related crime because the victims were gang members?

In a second ADW case, the defendant sometimes hung out with friends who were gang members, but he did not claim membership. He lived in an apartment complex that housed many gang members, so hanging with some of them seems reasonable, even for a non-member. He was sixteen years old and had no arrests. The assault charge resulted from a verbal confrontation; the defendant and his gang victim both claimed the other started the fight. Was this a gang-related incident?

Finally, we have a case in which members of two gangs were shouting at each other. This caused the driver of a car in the vicinity to swerve and crash, with the accident causing the driver's death. Can this accidental death be classified as gang related? The prosecution said yes; the defense said no.

3. *Motive-Defined Gang Crimes:* These cases are more straightforward. The first involves a "payback" homicide. The defendant's friend was killed, in his presence, by a rival gang. A week later, the defendant murdered one of the rivals. This is a gang-motivated crime.

The second case involves the driver of a car in which fellow gang members transported a captive rival gang member to an alley. While the defendant remained in the car, the others took the victim into the alley, beat him, and then poured gasoline over him and lit it. He died a horrible death. Although not in the alley, the defendant was intentionally involved and therefore charged with murder along with his co-defendants.

It was the victim's status as a rival gang member that yielded the motive-defined gang crime.

The third defendant is a female gang member who was involved in initiating a confrontation between two gangs. This resulted in a shooting, and she was charged with "aiding and abetting" the act. Again, it is the gang rivalry that triggered the motive definition.

Finally, we have the unusual case of a pre-emptive homicide. The defendant was a fringe member of a gang who shot a tagger he mistakenly believed to be a rival gang member. The shooter explained that he thought the victim had pointed a shotgun at him on a previous occasion. From the defendant's perspective, his act was in self-defense against a rival gang member—shoot first, ask questions later. Even though the victim was not a gang member, the gang-related motive was in the shooter's mind.

4. *Goal-Furtherance Gang Crimes:* Here we run into serious trouble. The prosecution often charges gang defendants with committing their acts "in furtherance of gang goals" or "at the direction of the gang." "Furtherance" is an ambiguous concept at best, easily overinterpreted by police and prosecutors to achieve an additional sentence in prison beyond that normally applied. My experience in these cases has been that too often the furtherance definition is not justifiable, but it derives from a tautology: a circular argument that if an act is gang related by member or motive definition, then it must also be in furtherance of gang goals. I offer three examples: The first fits the bill for the furtherance definition, while in my view the other two are very questionable.

The first is the case of a mentally deficient fourteen-year-old gang member from a dysfunctional family. He ran away from the scene when his friend and fellow member was shot by rival gang members. As a disciplinary measure imposed by an "OG" ("Original Gangster" or gang leader), he was told he must retaliate for this and another recent gang shooting. And so he did, being charged as a result with murder and attempted murder, with sentence enhancement for an act that was in furtherance of gang goals and at the direction of the gang. The act fits the definition perfectly, although the defense might well claim that the leader's command that the fourteen-year-old retaliate was a "mitigating factor," weakening the boy's responsibility for the act.

In the second case, the defendant was also charged with goal furtherance, but only because the prosecution used the circular reasoning that any gang member's offense must be for furtherance of gang goals. The defendant, a gang member, was arrested for possession of 2.38 grams of cocaine base carefully packaged into fifteen equal amounts. Clearly, the defendant was trafficking cocaine, not simply carrying around fifteen packages for his own use. In court, the police expert testified that the drug possession was in furtherance of gang goals—"for the benefit of the gang"—since, he said, the primary purpose of gangs included the possession of drugs for sale. The implication was that the profits of the sales would go back to the gang.

The defense, however, pointed out that there was no "gang treasury" and no other evidence that the defendant was selling on behalf of the gang instead of for his own financial gain. He was, the defense said, a drug trafficker, an entrepreneur working for himself. Criminological data by and large suggest that drug sales in such situations *are* individually motivated, regardless of whether or not the seller is gang involved. The assumption by the police expert and the prosecution was that any gang-connected crime is done *for* the gang, not only by a gang member. It's a false assumption.

The error in such reasoning is even more clear in our third case. The prosecution applied the gang-furtherance reasoning in an attempt to finish the criminal career of an inactive or former gang member. In the early morning, following drinks at a bar, the defendant and his girlfriend were driving home when they were stalled by a passing freight train at a rail crossing. While waiting for the long train to pass, the couple engaged in some very heavy petting, only to find that another couple had pulled alongside them in another car and was viewing the scene with some amusement. The defendant, embarrassed, drew his gun and deliberately fired a series of shots at the victims' car tires and rims, not at the victims themselves. The prosecution pursued the furtherance definition even though the victims were not gang members, no gang indicia (signs, challenges, names called, etc.) were used, and the location was miles from the defendant's former gang territory. It was a stupid, impulsive assault on the victims' tires done out of personal embarrassment. There were no gang implications beyond a possible member-defined act. But, again, the prosecution attempted the "because of gang, therefore for the purpose of the gang" ploy.

5. *Probable Non-Gang-Defined Crimes:* Let's look at one more set of three cases before moving on to other substantive issues in Part 2 of our street gang journey. These three raise the question of how we might look at our gang definitions generally.

In the first instance, the goal-furtherance law drafted specifically for street gangs was applied to the member of a prison gang. The law was not intended for this purpose—there is no mention of prison gangs in the legislation—and recall that our consensus definition offered earlier in Section 2 clearly excludes prison gangs. The law itself refers only to "criminal *street* gangs." In this particular case, the defendant was accused of involvement in a "hit" against another prison gang member. There was not even a hint of any prior street gang membership. The prosecution equated prison gang membership and goals with street gang membership and goals, quite deliberately, to get the added punishment available using the gang-goal-furtherance definition. Beware the misuse of definitions.

The second case provides quite an opposite example—an intragang rather than an intergang fight. At a gang party, a hard-core member of a well-known gang shot and killed a twenty-six-year-old former "O.G." who had "retired" from the gang after an earlier victimization had left him in a wheelchair. The prosecution wanted to exclude the defense's expert witness (me). This was done in two ways. First, the prosecutor referred to the gang as "your youth neighborhood association or group," avoiding the term "gang" and thereby questioning the relevance of a gang expert. Second, the prosecutor claimed that since it was an internal group affair, it did not involve rival gangs and could not be called a gang killing. The judge, obviously either ignorant of gang matters or in sympathy with the prosecution claims, bought both arguments. An obvious gang-member-defined killing (and the evidence might have shown it to be gang motive defined as well) was handled as a non-gang murder. What is not clear is why the prosecution was so anxious to exclude the defense expert by misuse of the definition.

Finally, we have the unusual case—group C in Section 2—in which the deputy sheriff came upon some taggers spray painting a neighborhood wall. He shot at them, and he was charged with gang-related felony ADW. He was not a gang member, nor were the taggers, so not even the broad member definition should have been involved. But it was, in yet another case of definitional misuse.

In sum, we have now looked at the use (or misuse) of various street gang definitions where they may count most—in court, where people's lives and futures can be determined. And we know from the other sections of Part 1 that the definitional issue also affects what we say about where gangs exist, how many gangs and gang members exist, and who can properly be labeled a gang member. Definitions are not "merely academic"; they affect our understanding and our actions. In the gang arena in particular, the definitional issues are important because of the ambiguities and the stereotypes that are so prevalent. We are in a good position, now, to move on to Part 2, where we can consider the broader contexts for understanding gangs and how over several decades we have come to understand them.

SPECIAL QUESTION: If several definitions of gangs or gang members or gang crimes exist, can there ever be a "science" of gangs?

PART 2 | Three Contexts for
Understanding Gangs

SECTION 5 | GANG PROCESSES AND STRUCTURES

Regardless of definitions, it is clear that over my tenure in the gang world:

> Gang cities have become far more plentiful,
>
> Gangs have become far more plentiful,
>
> Gang members have become far more plentiful, and
>
> Gang crimes have become far more plentiful.

One can note some other changes as well. A lot more research has been undertaken about street gangs, by an ever-expanding variety of researchers. At the same time, more attempts have been undertaken at gang control, including prevention, intervention, and law enforcement programs. And despite these two changes, more misinformation about street gangs has been spread and accepted, thanks principally to portrayals in the media—the movies, television, and the written press. Somehow the gaps between what can be known and what has been accepted as truth have actually widened. The sections of Part 2 will attempt to fill a few of these gaps.

There is more to be said about street gangs than the facts about their locations, numbers, and illegal behaviors. We need to consider what makes them special (Section 5), whether they are unique to our American world (Section 6), and what this implies about controlling them (Section 7). Finally, I want to add some brief notes (Section 8) on how I would spend my next ten years on gangs.

We start by asking what makes street gangs unique as groups, different from other groups of youth. The answer lies first in what I will call *group processes* and second in what I will call *gang structures*. Let's look first at the unique processes.

Street gangs don't emerge full-blown overnight. Rather, they develop through the processes of youthful relationships as young people interact in schools and neighborhoods. At least four such processes seem pivotal.

• *Social Marginalization:* With some exceptions, street gang members come from social, ethnic, or national minorities. In the United States, this means primarily African-American and Hispanic populations. In Western Europe, as we will see in Section 6, it means refugee and immigrant populations from a variety of East Asian, North African, Eastern European, and other countries. In both cases, it is not the specific minority population that is important, but rather the minority status itself. A small portion of these groups, given less than full acceptance by the majority population, end up as the fodder for gang formation, getting identity and a sense of belonging from their perceived mutual exclusion from mainstream society. The initial bonds of the gangs derive from the response to exclusions.

• *Oppositional Culture:* As articulated originally by Moore and Vigil (1989), street gangs develop a group-oriented attitude—the "oppositional culture"—that serves to cement their group bonds, their cohesiveness, by reacting negatively to outside intrusions and twisting them into self-justifying values. For instance, attempts to provide social services for gangs (job training, outreach workers, legal aid, etc.) are reinterpreted by gang members as proving how "special" and different they are from members of other groups. Or law enforcement efforts to crack down on gang members are reinterpreted to provide a mutual enemy, thus reinforcing group bonds within the gang. Whatever is done either for or against the gang is done with a pro-social message that is then distorted by the gang into an antisocial message, that the gang is special, strong, high status. The message received is distorted from the message intended; the stronger the message sent, whether by services or crackdowns, the greater the distortion into a message received that strengthens gang bonds.

- *The "Tipping Point"*: Street gangs, when they start, form from other groups (play groups, school groups, tagger crews, etc.) or in opposition to other groups that seem threatening. Yet most youth groups do *not* become street gangs. Most readers of this book probably belonged to informal as well as formal groups of youth, but few of the readers will claim gang membership. One of the principal dividing lines is the tipping point of illegal behavior.

When a youth group gets seriously involved in or simply oriented toward delinquent or criminal activities, it recognizes this about itself. While it may say to an outside inquiry, "Naw, man, we a social club," it knows better. It knows (technically, its members know) that its illegal thoughts and actions separate it from the other youth groups: "Yeah, we a gang; we do what we do (stealing, fighting, graffiti, etc.) and don't no one mess with us." Furthermore, community residents, school authorities, and the police also recognize that the group has crossed over the line and has become a gang. Once having crossed the line, a street gang will have a hard time moving back from the tipping point;

the gang identity has been established, as noted by the last defining factor in our street gang definition, "whose involvement in illegal behavior is part of their identity."

• *Violence as Unifier:* Even beyond the tipping point of illegal involvement, the issue of violence emerges as pivotal to gang members' identity with their groups. It's not that there's a lot of violence in gangs. To the contrary, violent offending is a small part of the overall crime pattern; there's far more property crime, vice (drugs, sex, alcohol), and "status offending" (truancy, running away, disobedience of parents, and so on). And all these crimes are themselves a small part of gang members' daily activities (sleeping, eating, school and work, and just hanging around).

So, in context, violence is relatively minor. But in serving the mythology and identity of the gang, it is major. It always has been so, as noted in both classical gang literature (Yablonsky 1963; Short and Strodtbeck 1965; Klein 1971) and modern gang literature (Sanchez-Jankowski 1991; Decker and Van Winkle 1996; Vigil 2002). Violence in the gang is as much storytelling and braggadocio as it is action, but either way it is a unifying theme. For the members, it sets themselves and their gang apart from all others; "heart," "courage," "cojones," "watching the other guy's back," and "we take no shit" are all statements of violence potential and commitment, regardless of the amount of violence actually undertaken. The bark is greater than the bite, but only because the bite is always possible, and sometimes taken.

Why are these four group processes so important? Because they make the gang a qualitatively different kind of group, not just a collection of kids who on occasion commit delinquent acts. These processes yield gang cohesiveness; in understanding gangs they trump ethnicity (Sanchez-Jankowski 1991; Vigil, 2002; Klein, 1995), and they trump neighborhood differences (Hall, Thornberry, and Lizotte, 2005).

Together, these processes lead to dramatically elevated levels of crime generally, and violence specifically. If we want to understand street gangs or if we want to attempt to control them, we must appreciate what goes on within them.

Another point is important to appreciate about both group processes in gangs and gang structure: Street gang leadership has both a stereotypical, mythical reputation and a far less dramatic reality. The strong, manipulative, violent leaders are the stereotype. Such leaders exist in some gangs, at some times—in police parlance, they are often known as "shot callers"—but they are not common and not typical.

Leadership in street gangs tends to be age related and clique related. It also tends to be as much functional as structural. That is, some gang members have influence because of their criminal propensities, but others have it because of their skills in sports or in social activities, or because of their verbal skills, which allow them to articulate gang values and perceptions. A single leader is uncommon; many influential members is the more common pattern.

There is practical importance in these descriptions. For instance, breaking up the gang by arresting high-crime leaders usually has little effect. Turning the gang around by resocializing or transforming high-reputation members usually also has little effect. The group trumps its own "leaders." Leadership gaps and influence gaps are filled by other members; the group carries on.

Let's consider group or gang cohesiveness for a moment. Cohesiveness is a group process that refers to the bonding between members and the strength of their commitment to each other and to the gang as an entity. In most gangs, overall cohesiveness is of only moderate strength. It can ebb and flow in response to both outside pressures and inside needs of the members. We can distinguish between "commitment to the gang" (an identity issue) and "reliance on one's clique" (a more personal kind of bonding). Large gangs are really affiliations of smaller cliques, and one has to appreciate both levels of involvement, in the overall gang and in one's clique within it. Gang cohesiveness is a function of both overall gang identity and clique loyalty.

Cliques, the smaller friendship groupings, can be based on similar residence, school attendance, family connection, age and gender, behavioral interests (from sports to crime), and so on. Also involved, of course, are shared past experiences, both positive and negative. Yet not all gang members are clique affiliated. For instance, in a large gang I studied for eighteen months, the Latins, 64 percent were core members (more likely to be in cliques), and only 26 percent were fringe members (less likely to be in cliques) over a measurement period of six months. The remainder couldn't be classified either way, and—more to the point—over half of all the gang members were not clique affiliated at all during that period. The general stereotype of gang members corresponds to the core members, yet as these figures demonstrate, the stereotype fits quite poorly. Street gangs are surprisingly loose-knit collectivities, and no one approach to gang control or gang crime reduction is likely to fit all.

The relationship between gang cohesiveness and crime levels is a dynamic one, with direct relevance to gang crime reduction. Increasing cohesiveness creates crime amplification, but crime and identity are mutual reinforcers. Anything—including many interventions and law enforcement actions against the gang—can yield increased cohesiveness and crime. Anything interrupting this cycle can be helpful. We don't want to "attack" gangs only to see the oppositional culture and the crime tipping point accelerated. When considering gang control then, it helps to understand these group processes so that, as in the medical warning, "first, do no harm."

One final point on this score deserves comment because it, too, affects how one approaches gang control. There is no *one* form of street gang. Gangs can be large or small, long term or short term, more or less cohesive, more or less territorial, more or less criminally involved, and so on. If one treats all gangs as being the same, then the treatment will often be wrong, perhaps even making things worse. Whether there are two types of gangs or ten is probably less important than the fact that there are several types. It is the fact of gang diversity itself that should make us cautious about generalizing too quickly about their nature.

I've indicated earlier that typing gangs by their ethnic or racial make-up doesn't work well. Group process trumps ethnicity, making the cross-ethnic differences far less notable than the similarities. However, my colleague Cheryl Maxson and I *have* been able to find gang types, five of them, by analyzing certain of their structural characteristics.[1] Using data on 2,860 gangs in 201 cities throughout the United States, we have shown "traditional" and "neotraditional" gangs to be the largest, longest-enduring, and most crime-producing gangs. They are not the most common form, but they best fit the media stereotype of large inner-city gangs with strong intergang rivalries and violent tendencies.

"Compressed" gangs, primarily adolescent groups of 50 to 100 members and less than ten years' duration, are the most common, found in both large and small cities. Least common are "collective" gangs, rather amorphous, but large collections with little internal structure, sometimes held together by loose neighborhood ties and extensive drug dealing (see Fleisher 1998 for a description of a collective gang in Kansas City). The smallest in size of our five types, but the most tightly structured, is the "specialty" gang, which is not versatile like the other four types, but rather manifests a narrow pattern of criminal behavior. Drug gangs, robbery or burglary gangs, car theft gangs, and skinheads are common examples.

These five types were derived from police interviews and data—not always the most reliable source of gang data—but then independently validated over several years in a very wide state survey (Illinois), in a nationwide survey, and by application to a number of gang descriptions from Western Europe.

Because gang membership turns over rather rapidly while the gang as a unit remains quite stable, this typology offers a consistent mechanism for conceptualizing what gangs are all about. We can understand gangs as a stable phenomenon, even as their membership changes. As an analogy, consider how certain college football teams remain powerful over many years—Miami, Florida State, Nebraska, Michigan, Texas, U.S.C.—even though no player is active for more than four years. Further, our research shows that from 75 to 95 percent of all street gangs fall into one of the five types, so if we could devise ways to control each type differentially, we could control most gangs. That may seem like pie in the sky, but it's certainly a goal worth pursuing (see Klein and Maxson 2006—especially Chapter 8).

CHARACTERISTICS OF FIVE STREET GANG TYPES

Type	Sub-groups	Size	Age Range	Duration	Territorial	Crime Versatility	Number in 201 Cities
Traditional	Yes	Average 180	Wide (20–30 years)	Long (>20 years)	Yes	Yes	316
Neotraditional	Yes	Average 75	No Pattern	Short (<10 years)	Yes	Yes	686
Compressed	No	Average 35	Narrow (<10 years)	Short (<10 years)	No Pattern	Yes	1,111
Collective	No	Average 55	Medium-Wide (>10 years)	Medium (10–15 years)	No Pattern	Yes	264
Specialty	No	Average 25	Narrow (<10 years)	Short (<10 years)	Yes	No	483

SPECIAL QUESTION: Why are group processes especially important in studying gangs?

ENDNOTE

1. I am summarizing here some extensive research reported in Chapter 5 of Klein and Maxson (2006), as well as elsewhere in less detail.

| **STREET GANGS HERE AND THERE**

T he previous five sections reflect experience with street gangs in America. Gangs elsewhere, it seemed, either didn't exist or had not been subjected to much research attention. But in the mid-1990s, with a sabbatical leave in Stockholm and a travel grant to visit other European cities, I picked up hints of new gang problems in London, Manchester, Berlin, Frankfurt, Stuttgart, and Kazan (Russia), as well as my home base in Stockholm. Were these merely scattered instances or signs of a new pattern of street gang proliferation?

To find out, I met with a few American and European colleagues during a conference in Belgium in 1997. The consensus in the group was that there was, indeed, an emerging problem and that it should be investigated. This was followed by a series of eight workshops, eventually involving well over 100 participants, in order in Germany, Norway, Belgium, and The Netherlands; then twice more in Germany; and finally in the United States, and Spain. These meetings, the two books and many research reports emanating from them, the adoption of our consensus Eurogang definition of gangs, and the development of several gang research instruments applicable across nations constitute the substance of what has come to be known as the Eurogang program.[1]

Section 6 describes some of the findings from this program for several reasons. First, the Eurogang program represents part of my forty-year journey in chasing the gang world. Second, the findings are interesting in their own light. Third, and most important, we can now look at both American and European street gangs to understand far better what is generic or common across nations and to understand as well some of the variations one finds within the generic patterns.

Let's start off with a matching exercise to get into the spirit of things and then apply what was described in Sections 1 through 5 to the Eurogang situation. The program has identified, to date, about 50 locations that have experienced street gang problems starting in 1980 or more recently. Of these, I've listed below 17 cities and countries alphabetically, followed by a series of questions about them. Look at the locations first, and consider what you may already know, or have heard, about them. Then move to the questions and try to fill in the appropriate location numbers. Some location numbers may appear more than once, and some not at all.

1. Belgium	7. France	13. Manchester
2. Berlin	8. Frankfurt	14. The Netherlands
3. Denmark	9. Genoa	15. Oslo
4. Edinburgh	10. Germany	16. Sweden
5. England	11. Kazan	17. Teubingen
6. Finland	12. London	

1. In what countries has the existence of street gangs been officially denied, despite clear police evidence of their presence?

   Answer:

2. In what city has the greatest ethnic and national diversity of street gang membership been reported?

   Answer:

3. Where in Western Europe have gangs been formed among the children of former citizens of Eastern Europe?

   Answer:

4. Where have immigrants from the southern part of the country formed street gangs in the northern part?

   Answer:

5. Where have traditional gangs been reported?

   Answer:

6. Where have specialty skinhead gangs been reported?

   Answer:

7. Where have traditional street gangs evolved into full-fledged adult criminal gangs?

   Answer:

8. Where are the street gangs limited to indigenous (i.e., local, non-minority) populations?

   Answer:

9. Where is one most likely to find street gangs comprised mostly of Algerian, Turkish, Moroccan, and Jamaican origin?

Answers: Algerian—

               Turkish—

               Moroccan—

               Jamaican—

10. Where is one most likely to find street gangs of Asian origin?

Answer:

Once you're provided some answers, read on and we'll take them one by one.

1. Public officials and academics in Belgium, England, and Sweden steadfastedly denied their gangs' existence in the late 1990s. England and Sweden have now altered their positions under pressure from both the police and the media.

2. Surprisingly, Oslo has reported the greatest diversity, including Norwegian, Pakistani, Somali, Iranian, Vietnamese, and Filipino groups. The core of one particular gang consisted of Somalis, Pakistanis, Moroccans, Turks, Vietnamese, and Norwegians (Lien 2001).

3. These gangs are found in the university town of Teubingen, Germany, and in other cities settled by "aussiedlers." These are the children of mostly Russian parents of German descent; technically, they are German citizens, but are seen as Russians who speak no German. They are doubly marginalized in their new setting made available after the collapse of East Germany (Weitekamp 2001).

4. Gangs in housing developments in Genoa, Italy, comprise youth from southern Italy—Calabria and Sicily. Their culture and experiences lead them to be almost the equivalent of a non-native minority in northern Italian cities (Gatti, Angelini, Marengo, Melchiorre, and Sasso 2005).

5. Traditional gangs require fifteen or twenty years to develop and are therefore scarce in Europe. I found them in Berlin (arising in opposition to attacking skinhead groups) and they are reported in Kazan and other Russian cities in the Volga region (Salagaev 2001).

6. Skinheads pop up here and there, but most notoriously in Denmark, England, Norway, and Sweden.

7. Salagaev (2001) provides a frightening picture of the evolution of traditional street gangs in Kazan into racketeering criminal groups, which strong-arm local citizens, extort businessmen, and seriously corrupt public officials since the collapse of the Soviet Union.

8. While the majority of European gang-involved locations report immigrant- and refugee-based street gangs, gangs limited to indigenous populations are reported in Edinburgh, Finland, and Kazan. The last of these presents a definitional problem because gang members tend to be Tatars, described by one Russian scholar as indigenous and by another as an ethnic minority in Russia (if not in Kazan).

9. Immigrant- and refugee-based street gangs reflect major demographic patterns in their "host" countries, and these differ substantially. Thus we find many Algerians in France, Moroccans in The Netherlands, Turks in Germany, and Jamaicans in London (called "Afro-Caribbeans" there).

10. This last was a bit of a trick question for American readers. We associate the term "Asian" with China, Korea, and Japan, principally. In London, Chinese and Indian gangs, and some Pakistani gangs as well, are referred to as Asians.

As can be seen from the foregoing, Europe presents a very diverse gang picture. And yet European gangs have much in common with American gangs, so I'll provide here some quick summaries of what has been learned. The interested reader can refer for details to the chapters in the two books produced by the Eurogang program (Klein, Kerner, Maxson, and Weitekamp, 2001; Decker and Weerman, 2005). Let's go section by section as set out in this book.

PROLIFERATION

To date, members of the Eurogang program have reported evidence of street gangs in fifty cities in sixteen countries. It is, thus, a scattered phenomenon, with most cities *not* classified as gang involved. Yet this fifty-city proliferation is recent and dramatic when compared with what was known in 1980. In the United States, only fifty-eight cities reportedly had gangs in 1960 (Klein 1995)—none could have predicted the explosion to 4,000 jurisdictions in the mid-1990s. This is no time for European nations to deny their gang problem.

DEFINITION

One of several reasons for early European denial of gangs was what we called the "Eurogang paradox." It goes like this:

A. Gangs, they say, are large, highly structured, territorial, violent groups like the Crips and Bloods, Latin Kings, Black Gangster Disciples, and White Fence.

B. Our European cities do not have such *West Side Story* groups, so we don't have street gangs.

C. But the paradox is that most American gangs don't fit this stereo-type either.

D. Therefore, maybe Europe does have gangs—the stereotype yields false conclusions. When we look for smaller, less structured, less violent groups of youth in trouble with the law, it seems we do in fact have street gangs in Europe.

Recognition of the paradox led to more careful scrutiny of troublesome youth groups, the recognition that they resembled the majority of American gangs, and the necessity of arriving at a gang definition that encompassed similar groups on both sides of the Atlantic. Thus, we arrived at the consensus Eurogang definition that is described in Section 2 of this book, allowing us to specify which groups could properly be labeled "street gang" and also which groups should not be so labeled.[2]

GANG MEMBERS

A review of available research reports from Europe certainly reinforces the idea of a generic pattern of street gangs. The similarities to U.S. gangs are far more striking than the differences.

- Both European and American gangs are composed principally, although not exclusively, of ethnic, national, or racial minorities. Our blacks, Hispanics, and Asians are matched by their Moroccan, Algerian, Turkish, "Asian," and Eastern European immigrants and refugees. Thus, we learn that it is not the specific background that is important, but the marginalization of these minority groups from the mainstream of society. If the majority-minority gaps increase, expect the gang levels to increase.

- Gangs on both continents tend to be made up of adolescents and very young adults. The relative absence of traditional gangs in Europe is associated with fewer adult gang members and is due to the relative recency of gangs in Europe.

- Females are found in both sets of gangs, although probably less commonly in Europe.

- As is the case in the United States, crime is far higher among European gang members than among non-gang youth. The levels are lower in Europe, but reveal the same versatile pattern. Gang members do a little of everything in both Europe and the United States: property crimes predominate.

- In both settings, gang members are hard to stereotype because they show much variation in personalities, skills, family backgrounds, and so on. Indeed, the variations are broad enough that there is much overlap on these characteristics between gang and non-gang youth from the same neighborhoods. Gangs, as has been noted, are qualitatively different from non-gang groups, but gang members are less qualitatively different from their non-gang peers.

- What is not yet determined, however, is whether or not the risk factors for joining gangs in America, as listed in Section 3 of this book, are the same in European countries. Here is an opening for some creative research to be undertaken.

GANG CRIME

As noted above, European gang crime exhibits a versatile pattern overall, rather than specializing in violence, or drug distribution, or intimidation, as the picture so often emerges in media reports. In this, European and American patterns are similar.

Also similar is the fact that gang-related crime is far more extensive than non-gang crime. This was the consistent report from a gathering of Eurogang researchers in Albany, New York, in 2004 and also becomes clear when one reviews the reports of the relatively low levels of European non-gang violence revealed by the International Self-Report Delinquency Study (ISRD: see Junger-Tas, Terlouw, and Klein 1994; Junger-Tas, Marshall, and Ribeaud 2003).

More interesting, perhaps, is the comparison of crime rates between European and U.S. gangs, since this is where differences emerge.

Overall, gang crime levels among European gangs are somewhat lower than in the United States (even though they are still higher than non-gang levels). In most, but not all, of the reports from the Eurogang program, homicide gets no mention at all; lethal violence is low.

Two factors seem clearly related to this. First, firearms are far less accessible in most European countries than they are in the United States. Almost 95 percent of all gang-related homicides in the United States are caused by firearms. Second, the sense of territoriality—the defense of one's "turf"—seems less common in European settings. Since territoriality and intergang rivalries account for much of the gang homicide pattern in the United States, it makes sense that fewer violent confrontations will occur in Europe. Fewer confrontations plus lower firearm accessibility yield far fewer gang-related deaths in European gang settings.

GROUP PROCESSES AND GANG STRUCTURES

After one overcomes the "Eurogang paradox," which incorrectly denies American-style gangs in Europe, it becomes apparent in reading European gang research reports that the same group processes found in American gangs are found in European gangs as well. The social marginalization of minority populations is a strong precursor to street gang formation. The oppositional culture that develops in these groups is common on both sides of the ocean. The role of criminal activity in providing a "tipping point" from youth group to street gang is common as well.

A significant difference may exist, however, in the degree to which violence serves as a unifying theme within European gangs. The lower violence level there (although it is higher than among non-gang groups) may—and this is pure speculation at this point—yield somewhat lower cohesiveness among the European gangs. If so, there is more hope there for successful interventions and control programs that do not inadvertently increase gang cohesiveness. Nonetheless, it seems clear that the usual group processes that make American street gangs qualitatively different from other groups perform much the same functions in Europe. Group processes lead to increased cohesiveness and the amplification of criminal pursuits, as empirically demonstrated in such disparate locations as Edinburgh (Bradshaw 2005) and Kazan (Salagaev 2001).

So far, it appears that all five types of street gangs identified in the United States—traditional, neotraditional, compressed, collective, and specialty gangs—appear in Europe also. However, they do so in different proportions. Traditional gangs are, as yet, uncommon. Collective gangs are rare. Neotraditional, compressed, and specialty gangs are most common. This applicability of the American typology, even with the different proportions, joins the similarities in gang processes to confirm the impression that various types of street gangs, wherever they develop, have far more in common than they have dissimilarities. A generic street gang *phenomenon* exists, which means that generic *knowledge* about gangs also exists. It may be, therefore, that common approaches to gang control can be devised, so we turn to this issue in the next section.

SPECIAL QUESTION: If American and European street gangs are similar, can we expect the same in Central America, Africa, and Asia?

ENDNOTES

1. A summary statement of the program can be found in Klein (2002). The books containing many of the original gang research reports are Klein, Kerner, Maxson, and Weitekamp (2001) and Decker and Weerman (2005).

2. On the nature of non-gang groups in Europe, interesting and varied descriptions are offered by Gruter and Versteegh (2001), Kersten (2001), Dekleva (2001), and Sarnecki and Pettersson (2001).

SECTION 7 | STREET GANG CONTROL

T his journey through the evolving world of street gangs has involved two progressions, one through time and the other through growth in knowledge. There should, therefore, be a third progression—advances in understanding how to control gangs. The time perspective has seen enormous progression, from street gangs as "play groups" in Chicago (Thrasher 1927; Maxson and Klein 2002) to the several types of criminally involved gangs described in Section 5. The knowledge progression has been even greater, as more and more researchers have added information about the nature of gang behaviors, members, and contexts, as summarized throughout this volume, to the knowledge base.

There has been change as well in our approaches to gang control, although I am loathe to characterize these changes as "progression" or growth. We've tried a lot of approaches; it is not clear that we have learned much about *successful* approaches. Through the 1950s, the emphasis was on finding ways to involve local communities in responding to their own gang problems. The 1960s and 1970s turned predominantly to "detached worker" programs, in which street workers were assigned to establish rapport with gang members and connect (or reconnect) them with pro-social aspects of family, school, employment, and other social services.

As gang problems worsened and evidence for the success of community-based and social service programs failed to emerge, the 1980s and 1990s saw a predominant emphasis on law enforcement and penal approaches, eschewing prevention and social service in favor of deterrence and suppression of street gang proliferation and criminal activity. As you read these pages in the 21st century, the evidence favoring suppressive law enforcement programs has failed as well to demonstrate their value. Lip service is being given to some combination of enforcement and community involvement, but again with little evidence to date of an overall pattern of success. It makes sense, then, to look at several examples of gang control programs for which some success has in fact been claimed.

I use the phrase "gang control" in these remarks in a very general way. I mean it to include three general perspectives that have become the "lingua franca" of modern gang writings: prevention, intervention, and suppression.

Prevention refers roughly to those undertakings aimed at decreasing the likelihood of street gang formation and the risks of youth joining already existing gangs. Thus, one can point to community mobilization programs, recreational and service programs for kids at risk of gang joining, and educational programs designed to strengthen youths' life skills and resistance to gang recruitment.

Intervention generally refers to programs aimed at decreasing current gang activity and weaning individual members away from their gangs. Truce programs and conflict resolution projects are included here, as are most detached worker programs and agency agendas that offer job opportunities, educational enrichment, personal and family counseling, and legal help to youth already involved in gang life.

Suppression includes many law enforcement programs, especially those that go beyond the normal police and prosecution practices to which we are all subject. Specialized gang units can be found in police departments, prosecutors' offices, and correctional institutions. Specific anti-gang legislation seeks easier convictions and enhanced prison sentences for gang members, while civil gang injunctions provide special punishment for a list of behaviors, both illegal and legal, that the courts determine make local communities especially sensitive to or fearful of gang member activity.

Following are brief descriptions of six gang control programs for which claims of success in reducing street gang problems have been widely offered. They include two programs each in prevention, intervention, and suppression. I'll provide a hint—there has been some success associated with several of the six—but the readers' task is to consider each of them and estimate where such success most probably has been demonstrated. Don't cheat; make your estimates before reading beyond the six descriptions.

1. *L.A. Bridges I:* With an initial sum of close to $50 million, this prevention project was (and is, as I write this) located in 29 middle school areas of the city of Los Angeles. It attempted to bring together, in each area, local youth service agencies and lay groups to coordinate and develop comprehensive social service, recreational, and educational programs to serve designated numbers of at-risk youths. Initiated because of a highly publicized gang-related killing of a three-year-old girl, L.A. Bridges was empowered by the Los Angeles City Council specifically to keep kids from joining their local street gangs. L.A. Bridges also included a substantial sum of money to contract for an

independent evaluation of its success in reducing gang joining and gang crime.

2. *Gang Resistance Education and Training (G.R.E.A.T.):* The G.R.E.A.T. program, modeled after the D.A.R.E. program in drug use, was offered nationwide in seventh grade to "immunize" youth in the schools against involvement in gang activity. This prevention program employed uniformed police officers as teachers of a series of nine once-a-week lessons on life skills, peer pressures, cultural sensitivity, drugs, personal responsibility, and the like. Discussion about gang issues was included as seemed appropriate. Unlike L.A. Bridges, the G.R.E.A.T. program applied to all seventh graders in each school rather than being targeted at at-risk youth. Like L.A. Bridges, the program contracted for a large-scale, independent evaluation of its outcomes.

3. *The Group Guidance Project:* This was an intervention program run by the Los Angeles County Probation Department. It assigned officers as detached workers to four large, traditional black gangs in south central Los Angeles, involving about 800 male and female gang members over a four-year period. The workers met with segments of their gangs in weekly "club" meetings, organized numerous group activities (sports, car washes, dances, charm clinics, tutoring sessions, and so on), provided many hours of individual and family counseling, and made connections between the gang members and school, court, and employment institutions. There was, by design, a strong emphasis on group programming in order to deal with the gang as a unit and to get more spread of effect than would be achieved through individual contacts. Like our first two programs above, the Group Guidance Project had an independent evaluation built into it, funded in large part by the Ford Foundation.

4. *Community Youth Gang Services (C.Y.G.S.):* This, too, took place in Los Angeles, but over a twenty-year period. It, too, used a

form of detached worker program, but it was significantly different, being modeled after an earlier effort in Philadelphia. It was a detached worker program with a rather strong suppressive (or at least law enforcement) element built in. Instead of building rapport with gang members to help provide services to them, and instead of using group programming to reach gang members, C.Y.G.S. put its emphasis on conflict resolution, in coordination with the police. The workers responded to "hot spots" where police engaged gang members, using radio-dispatched cars. When the police completed their activity, the members had the duty of following through on tensions, resolving further disputes and rumors, and using community resources to reduce further confrontations. This was an unusual example of a suppression-oriented intervention. In its first year, C.Y.G.S. invited an independent evaluation team to assess its progress, and it was monitored in later years by city officials because it was a city-funded operation.

5. *Anti-gang Legislation: Sentence Enhancements:* Various forms of special anti-gang legislation have been passed at the state and federal levels, but the best known of these are modeled after California's Street Terrorism Enforcement and Prevention (S.T.E.P.) Act. In states adopting the model, gangs are defined generally as criminal groups of three or more, formal or informal, with names and signs, where members have committed such acts as murder, attempted murder, assault, drive-by shootings, robbery, arson, and witness intimidation. Thus, the legislation has a clear group emphasis and targets convictions for the most serious gang-stereotypical offenses. An individual shown in court to be a member of such a criminal group can be sentenced upon conviction to many additional years in prison.

The rationale here is based on the notion that gang membership constitutes a conspiracy to commit crime and that membership is in a group one of whose primary purposes is to commit serious crimes.

As you can see, this takes the definition of a street gang way beyond the consensus definition emphasized in this book, almost totally criminalizing any level of street gang membership and applying serious penalties for membership. Data on defendants charged, on convictions and sentences, and on the deterrence of other offenses are available for assessment in criminal justice files.

6. *Civil Gang Injunctions (C.G.I.s):* This second approach to gang suppression involves obtaining court orders prohibiting certain behaviors described as injurious to community safety. Within a specified area—a few blocks, a neighborhood, even a whole community— evidence is gathered to demonstrate that a specific gang constitutes a serious threat. This evidence is presented to the court and, if accepted, leads to a temporary restraining order and then an injunction against the gang members prohibiting a list of both illegal and otherwise legal behaviors. Enjoined gang members arrested for these behaviors within the designated geographical area can then be prosecuted for violation of the court order and fined or incarcerated accordingly. The injunction usually sets early curfews, and the enjoined legal behaviors typically include carrying pagers, hand-signaling or whistling at passing cars (suggesting drug sales), and associating with other gang members. Despite legal challenges to their constitutionality, appeals courts have generally upheld civil gang injunctions, citing the rights of the community over the rights of individual gang members. Few independent evaluations of C.G.I.s have been built in; most have been after-the-fact assessments.

Again, my challenge to the reader is to consider each of these six gang control approaches and decide which are more likely to have demonstrated some success in reducing gang problems. Your choices may indeed relate to the viability of each approach, but my guess is that the choices you make may more likely reflect your own values. Do you favor prevention? Intervention? Suppression? Do you define gang problems as basic community issues? Social service issues? Crime problems? I have found that most assumptions about gang control, and most beliefs in its effectiveness, are based not on data-based evaluation, but on conventional wisdom and ideology. We judge more by our values than by assessment of available evidence.

With this as a forewarning, we can look at our six programs for supportive evidence. It is important in doing so to keep in mind two basic issues. First, did the program *as designed* yield supportive evidence of success for its ideas? Second, was the program implemented well enough that it is even fair to assess those ideas? Evaluating a weak vaccine is unfair to the vaccine.[1]

L.A. Bridges developed evaluation procedures during its first year, but there was no follow-through on that. Purely administrative assessments provided no clear clues to effects on gang problems. Since part of the program was implemented in areas with relatively low gang involvement and since it targeted at-risk kids generally rather than those at risk of gang membership specifically, it is unlikely that it achieved reductions in gang activity. It may have been a good youth service program; it could not demonstrate any effect on gang membership or gang crime. Nevertheless, it has been continued for ten years largely because of its political appeal.

The G.R.E.A.T. program was subjected to a well-designed, multiyear evaluation across many locations in the United States. Although first indications were positive, the long-term follow-up was discouraging. Youth in classrooms with the program, when compared to those without the program, showed consistent, but very minor improvements in attitudes and perceptions, but absolutely no differences in gang joining and gang-related behavior. G.R.E.A.T. was a well-implemented program that slightly improved kids' life skills, but it did nothing for gang problems. This may be in part because its didactic curriculum was not well targeted at specifically gang-related values and perceptions and in part because it was applied to all seventh graders, most of whom would not have joined gangs in any case and who received no "booster" shots in later grades. It may be as well that having the curriculum taught by uniformed police officers created some credibility problems.

The Group Guidance Project successfully implemented a whole host of group activities for gang members. An extensive independent evaluation suggested that, inadvertently, this gang emphasis seemed to make the gangs even more attractive; they grew in size and became more cohesive. The result was a marked increase in gang-related offenses. When the detached workers were transferred or reduced their level of group programming, gang size, cohesiveness, and crime went down. The workers and their activities had become a fulcrum around which the large gangs coalesced. The Group Guidance Project, based on conventional social wisdom and a preventive ideology, not only failed to ameliorate the gang problem, but actually made it worse.

The C.Y.G.S., also a group-oriented program, but with a deterrence emphasis, did not have any evaluation worthy of the name. Its directors initially invited an independent assessment, but then consistently undermined the evaluation effort and soon abandoned it. Almost twenty years later, the city council disbanded C.Y.G.S. specifically because it had failed to demonstrate any effects. Ironically, the city council took the scheduled funding from this failed effort to support L.A. Bridges, a far more grandiose effort with a failed evaluation.

Anti-gang legislation, to this day, has failed to build in designed independent evaluations. A review of relevant issues with such legislation, both positive and negative (Bjerregaard 2003), suggests the problems probably equal the potential benefits. Given the rapid spread of anti-gang legislation and its unverified claims of success at both the state and the federal levels, independent assessment is clearly called for. Unfortunately, conventional wisdom and ideology seldom support objective attempts to investigate program outcomes.

Civil gang injunctions likewise have seldom invited evaluations as they were implemented. One, in Inglewood, California, was funded for an evaluation, but the program implementation was so poor that the evaluators could not support a positive outcome. Two after-the-fact evaluations provided mixed results. One suggested an increase in crime resulting from the injunction. Another, analyzing pooled police data from fourteen injunctions, found a 5 to 10 percent reduction in violent crime, but this was limited to assaults, with little effect on robbery and no effect on property crime. Still, a little success is better than none. A fourth evaluation concentrating not on crime, but on community reaction, found positive effects on community residents' perceptions of gang activity and program effectiveness. Since injunctions are justified by the courts by reference to the rights of community residents, this is a promising first finding in this realm. What is not clear is whether community residents felt better because attention was paid to their concerns, because gangs became less visible, or because crime was reduced.

Where does all this take us? The six programs discussed here were selected for illustrative purposes from about sixty discussed in *Street Gang Patterns and Policies* (Klein and Maxson 2006). The vast majority of these sixty were unevaluated and therefore of little use in the search for successful approaches. Maybe some of them were really good. Maybe some of them made things worse. Without competent evaluations, we just can't know.

Each of the six discussed here seemed at first to promise much. But L.A. Bridges (prevention), C.Y.G.S. (intervention), and anti-gang legislation (suppression) failed to mount useful evaluations. G.R.E.A.T.

(prevention), the Group Guidance Project (intervention), and civil gang injunctions (suppression) provided a mixed picture of no effect, negative effect, and slight positive effect. So long as social services practitioners, criminal justice officials, and politicians cling to their conventional, untested wisdom, they'll feel little pressure to account for the outcomes of their efforts. So long as they build programs to express rather than test their ideologies, they will actively resist independent evaluations. As the saying goes, "Don't confuse me with facts; my mind's already made up." Meanwhile, street gangs remain a national problem; older gang members are replaced by young gang members, and the costs to human safety of both gang and non-gang citizens continue unabated. The journey continues, and we must design our programs with careful, planned evaluations so we can increase the effectiveness of those programs.

SPECIAL QUESTION: Given past failures of gang control programs and what we now know about gangs, what general principles should guide development of new, more effective programs?

ENDNOTE

1. Readers wishing to read more about these programs and their evaluations can refer to more complete descriptions. For #1 and #2, see Klein and Maxson (2006). For #3, see Klein (1971). For #4 and #5, see Klein (1995). For #6, see Maxson, Hennigan, and Sloane (2005).

SECTION 8 | THE NEXT TEN YEARS

Although this book is based on forty years of exposure to gang issues, maybe I'm not through yet. I still get those phone calls:

- Dr. Klein, what's the nature of street gangs?
- Dr. Klein, aren't gangs just another kind of organized crime?
- Dr. Klein, are gangs getting worse?
- Dr. Klein, what should we do about gangs?
- Dr. Klein, what programs have worked to reduce gang problems?

Let me turn to a December 2004 call from a crime reporter in Los Angeles, my home base. He told me that all the residents of an apartment complex were being evicted, at the behest of the police and the city attorney, because some of the apartments had been used over a substantial period of time (residents in the area claim over twenty years) to sell drugs. Nine people, including two children, had been shot since June 2002. Gangs are blamed, he said; residents feel helpless. The landlord has been warned and advised to clean up the situation, but it still goes on.

"How can you tell if these dope dealers are gang members?" asks the reporter. "What does it mean to be a 'gang associate'?"

I tried to answer—indeed, readers of this book could provide some answers—but I wonder also how the police and city attorney have allowed this situation to fester for so long and what has kept the local community unable to respond effectively. And how is it that the non-drug-selling residents also get evicted? Where is community policing, in which residents and police actively collaborate to solve community problems? What provisions might be made, but haven't been, for the innocent, but victimized residents?

Media reports over the following weeks documented the grave situation in and around this apartment complex. Liberals and conservatives offered their conventional wisdoms about what should be done, and editorials spouted ideologies about poverty and discrimination, crime and terror. After forty years, it all sounded very familiar.

So I thought about those forty years and asked myself what I would do if I had an additional ten? My answers won't solve the apartment complex controversy, but maybe they will help us get there. Not surprisingly, they cover two areas, future research on gangs and suggestions for thinking about gang control. In the spirit of this book, I'll be brief.

RESEARCH ISSUES

1. We have, finally, learned enough about the few factors predicting who will and won't join street gangs (see Section 3) that this is now a direction for more focused research. I envision a set of projects that will take the risk factors identified in several longitudinal projects, as well as our own cross-sectional comparisons of gang and non-gang youth, and develop them into a predictive scale. This process involves several steps—known well to the research community—including

operationalizing the risk factors across sites, developing scale score values for each, and then applying the scale in several settings and cross-validating it. The value of such research lies both in its knowledge-building results and in its early identification of gang-prone youth for purposes of prevention of gang-joining processes.

2. The gang typology discussed in Section 5 deserves further testing for its stability over time and its applicability to different locations; I've already found it to be generally applicable to Western Europe, as well as the United States. Understanding the stable patterns of street gangs will help defeat the stereotyping of gangs now so common in both the criminological literature and the media. In addition, I'm convinced that different gang types (consider, for example, traditional versus specialty gangs) should be subjected to different, somewhat type-specific forms of gang control. Using the same technologies, whether social service or suppression, will be differentially useful and, in some cases, counterproductive.

3. I'd like to see more attention paid to finding ways to empower communities to handle their own gang problems. Reliance on the police is obviously not enough. Reliance on family-strengthening processes is obviously not enough, in the face of the power of peer influence in the streets. Useful research related to improving community efficacy has been undertaken, but it's a terribly complex process and deserves far more concentrated attention in different settings. Gangs don't emerge through spontaneous combustion. They are spawned, are fostered (often inadvertently), and can be controlled within their own environments. I'll come back to this issue in later pages.

4. Ethnographers doing street work, survey researchers using household and school surveys, researchers gathering gang data from knowledgeable adults (police, parents, agency personnel, and so on), and researchers extracting data from police and court files *necessarily* develop different images of gangs and gang members. I'd like to foster

research programs that deliberately and planfully study the *same* gangs using these different methods and sources of information. Such information would give us a more balanced and comprehensive image of the topic, and it would better alert us to the limitations and advantages of each method of data collection. Researchers, working in teams if necessary, need to become more multifaceted as opposed to advocating for their own preferred approaches.

5. Finally, as you might guess, I'd like to encourage far more *comparative* gang research—across gangs, across cities, and across nations. The Eurogang program is a strong start in this direction, but long-term expansion of such efforts is needed. It's a knowledge-building enterprise because, at the same time, it allows us to build generic or broad understandings of street gangs, as well as the patterned differences that exist within the commonalities. Even as these words are written, there is a great disquietude taking hold among public officials and the media about Central American gangs and their footholds in the United States. This rising concern should be met with knowledge gathering, not shoot-from-the-hip suppression activities, as is now happening.

CONTROL ISSUES

In the book *Street Gang Patterns and Policies* (2006), Cheryl Maxson and I have presented a broad spectrum of gang control goals and programs that are available for testing. I don't want to repeat that material here. I do, however, want to express my inclinations resulting from this forty-year journey.

Speaking very broadly, gang control can be approached on three levels: the societal, individual, and community levels. The societal level refers to such broad strokes as poverty, segregation, migration, racism, inequalities in educational and social services, and the like. Any gang scholar will acknowledge that social problems of this sort help to spawn street gangs, just as they impinge on levels of homelessness, mental health problems, drug abuse, and a host of other problems. Gang youth, marginalized from the central stream of society, fall through the social sieves that help to contain most of their peers.

Just to say this is not very useful for gang control purposes. Poverty, racism, and the like are not about to be solved in our society—certainly not in my next ten years. I can't foment a social revolution, nor it seems can the national Republican and Democratic Parties. We need to understand how societal-level problems feed our gang situations, but we can't very well change them (or at least haven't done so in the past).

A second level, and the one most commonly employed, is that of the individual gang member. In both prevention and intervention, we have attempted to alter the life paths of gang-prone youth. We have used individual counseling, legal aid, school tutoring, job training and location, recreation, mentoring, and a host of other modalities well known in youth services generally. There have been many success stories as individual would-be and actual gang members have been positively affected. And surely prevention of gang joining is far more efficient than is rehabilitation or reintegration of gang members. Yet we don't seem to have made much measurable headway in overall gang reduction. There are three reasons for this, I think. First, the gang member is not quite a typical youth, and his group is not a typical group. The group processes discussed in Section 5 overwhelm and obstruct our individual interventions. I am, perhaps unfairly, always reminded of the gang member for whom over a year and half we found ten jobs, psychological counseling, drug counseling, tattoo removal, and U.S. Marine Corps recruiting. He went through all of that before wounding an adolescent stranger, shooting to death an older adult, and then, in prison, killing another inmate. Sometimes we have to face the fact that we don't have sufficient leverage to alter the lives of committed gang members; therein lies the second problem with the individual level—we use our meager resources to change individual life trajectories that have been taking shape for fifteen or twenty years. Frankly, we're not up to the task in many, perhaps most, cases.

The third reason for failure to show measurable progress at the individual level is simply that there are too many gang members and not enough controllers. The NYGC has over the years offered estimates of gang members as high as 800,000, based on police reports made to it. Given that the police are often unaware of younger and female gang members, even the estimates offered are probably undercounts. Let's guess that the "real" figure (remember the definitional problems from Section 3) is closer to a million; there is simply no way we can respond to such a large number of hard-to-reach, marginalized youth. The individual level is inefficient at best, no matter how heartfelt and dedicated the efforts may be.

That brings us to the third level, that of the local neighborhood or community. This is where I'd put my money over the next ten years. I'd do so with the goals of reducing gang development, preventing gang joining, and controlling gang activity, all of which are more group-oriented than individual goals. It's the weakening of the gang as a unit that best deserves our attention. But that's easily said and not easily done. There's a long tradition of urban sociology and social policy that has attempted community empowerment around a host of issues. Street gangs have been the specific focus of several large attempts, but not with much to show for it. Organizing poorly organized communities is almost an oxymoron. Yet I'd still put my money here—well, someone's money, since I'm talking about scores of millions of dollars. I'd do so because the gang is, first and foremost, a community problem. It is the community's kids who decide whether or not to form or join gangs, and it is the community's residents, institutions, and businesses that are most victimized by gang activity.

I'll start with a meeting over several days of urban sociologists, a few anthropologists, some political scientists, and a few mayors and city managers. My colleagues and I can provide the gang knowledge, but the others will be charged with outlining the steps suggested by prior research that can lead to increasing community efficacy, the capacity of local communities to take charge of their own problems. From that meeting and subsequent gatherings must emerge several blueprints for getting the gang problem in the hands of newly responsive communities and for sustaining the effort over many years.

Pie in the sky, you say? Yeah, but show me where we've done better. There's one final ideal goal: evaluate, evaluate, evaluate. I am tired of gang prevention, intervention, and suppression projects that don't build in competent, sustained, independent assessments of their impacts. We should be accountable for the money we spend on gang control efforts, especially given some projects that appear to have made things worse. My desired community improvement programs would have to include adequate evaluations. Otherwise, I'd take the money and run.

SELECTED SUPPLEMENTAL READINGS

This book draws heavily on the three books at the head of the list below, but these in turn are based on a great deal of work by other authors over the years. Included in the list are recent original monographs, comprehensive summaries, and even summaries of summaries, since street gang knowledge has now become quite extensive. Most *original* gang research is published as journal articles or chapters in edited books. References to those are included in the books listed here, and serious students of street gangs are encouraged to seek out these original research reports.

Klein, M.W., and C.L. Maxson. 2006. *Street gang patterns and policies.* Oxford, England: Oxford University Press.

Klein, M.W. 2004. *Gang cop: The words and ways of Officer Paco Domingo.* Walnut Creek, Calif.: AltaMira Press.

Klein, M.W. 1995. *The American street gang: Its nature, prevalence, and control.* Oxford, England: Oxford University Press.

Covey, H.C., S. Menard, and R.J. Franzese. 1997. *Juvenile gangs.* 2nd ed. Springfield, Ill.: Charles C. Thomas.

Decker, S.H., and B. Van Winkle. 1996. *Life in the gang.* New York: Cambridge University Press.

Decker, S.H., and F.M. Weerman, eds. 2005. *European street gangs and troublesome youth groups: Findings from the Eurogang research program.* Walnut Creek, Calif: AltaMira Press.

Fleisher, M.S. 1998. *Dead end kids: Gang girls and the boys they know.* Madison: University of Wisconsin Press.

Hagedorn, J.M. 1998. *People and folks; Gangs, crime, and the underclass in a Rustbelt city.* 2nd ed. Chicago: Lake View Press.

Huff, C.R., ed. 1990, 1996, 2001. *Gangs in America.* 1st, 2nd, and 3rd eds. Thousand Oaks, Calif.: Sage.

Klein, M.W., H-J. Kerner, C.L. Maxson, and E.G.M. Weitekamp, eds. 2001. *The Eurogang paradox: Street gangs and youth groups in the U.S. and Europe.* Dordrecht/Boston: Kluwer Academic Publishers.

Miller, J. 2001. *One of the guys: Girls, gangs, and gender.* New York: Oxford University Press.

Miller, J., C.L. Maxson, and M.W. Klein, eds. 2001. *The modern gang reader.* 2nd ed. Los Angeles: Roxbury Press.

Moore, J.W. 1991. *Going down to the barrio: Homeboys and homegirls in change.* Philadelphia: Temple University Press.

Spergel, I.A. 1995. *The youth gang problem: A community approach.* New York: Oxford University Press.

Thornberry, T.P., M.D. Krohn, A.J. Lizotte, C.A. Smith, and K. Tobin. 2003. *Gangs and delinquency in developmental perspective.* New York: Cambridge University Press.

Vigil, J.D. 1988. *Barrio gangs: Street life and identity in Southern California.* Austin: University of Texas Press.

REFERENCES

Bjerregaard, Beth. 2003. Antigang legislation and its potential impact: The promises and pitfalls. *Criminal Justice Policy Review* 14, no. 2: 171–192.

Bradshaw, Paul. 2005. Terrors and young teams. In *European street gangs and troublesome youth groups: Findings from the Eurogang research program*, edited by Scott H. Decker and Frank M. Weerman. Walnut Creek, Calif.: AltaMira Press.

Brett, Rachel, and Irma Specht. 2004. *Young soldiers: Why they choose to fight.* Boulder, Colo.: Lynne Rienner.

Corrections Management Quarterly. 2001. Responding to the threat of gangs: Leadership and management strategies. 5, no. 1 (winter).

Covey, Herbert C., Scott Menard, and Robert J. Franzese. 1997. *Juvenile gangs.* 2nd ed. Springfield, Ill.: Charles C. Thomas.

Decker, Scott H. 2001. The impact of organizational features on gang activities and relationships. In *The Eurogang paradox: Street gangs and youth groups in the U.S. and Europe*, edited by Malcolm W. Klein, Hans-Juergen Kerner, Cheryl L. Maxson, and Elmar G.M. Weitekamp. Dordrecht/Boston: Kluwer Academic Publishers.

Decker, Scott H., and Barrik Van Winkle. 1996. *Life in the gang.* New York: Cambridge University Press.

Decker, Scott H., and Frank M. Weerman, eds. 2005. *European gangs and troublesome youth groups.* Walnut Creek, Calif.: AltaMira Press.

Dekleva, Bojan. 2001. Gang-like groups in Slovenia. In *The Eurogang paradox: Street gangs and youth groups in the U.S. and Europe*, edited by Malcolm W. Klein, Hans-Juergen Kerner, Cheryl L. Maxson, and Elmar G.M. Weitekamp. Dordrecht/Boston: Kluwer Academic Publishers.

Egley, Arlen, Jr., James C. Howell, and Celine K. Major. 2004. Recent patterns of gang problems in the United States. In *American youth gangs at the millennium*, edited by Finn-Aage Esbensen, Stephen G. Tibbets, and Larry Gaines. Long Grove, Ill.: Waveland Press.

Fearn, Noelle E., Scott H. Decker, and G. David Curry. 2001. Public policy responses to gangs: Evaluating the outcomes. In *The modern gang reader.* 2nd ed. edited by Jody Miller, Cheryl L. Maxson, and Malcolm W. Klein. Los Angeles: Roxbury Press.

Fleisher, Mark. 1998. *Dead end kids: Gang girls and the boys they know.* Madison: University of Wisconsin Press.

Gatti, Uberto, Francesca Angelini, Gilberto Marengo, Natalia Melchiorre, and Marcello Sasso. 2005. An old-fashioned youth gang in Genoa. In *European street gangs and troublesome youth groups: Findings from the Eurogang research program*, edited by Scott H. Decker and Frank M. Weerman. Walnut Creek, Calif.: AltaMira Press.

Gruter, Paul, and Peter Versteegh. 2001. Toward a problem-oriented approach to youth groups in The Hague. In *The Eurogang paradox: Street gangs and youth groups in the U.S. and Europe*, edited by Malcolm W. Klein, Hans-Juergen Kerner, Cheryl L. Maxson, and Elmar G.M. Weitekamp. Dordrecht/Boston: Kluwer Academic Publishers.

Hall, Gina Pedley, Terence P. Thornberry, and Alan J. Lizotte. 2005. The gang facilitation effect and neighborhood risk: Do gangs have a stronger influence on delinquency in disadvantaged areas? In *Studying youth gangs*, edited by James F. Short, Jr., and Lorine A. Hughes. Walnut Creek, Calif.: AltaMira Press.

Junger-Tas, Josine, Ineke Haen Marshall, and Denis Ribeaud. 2003. *Delinquency in international perspective: The international self-reported delinquency study (ISRD)*. The Hague: Kugler Publications.

Junger-Tas, Josine, Gert-Jan Terlouw, and Malcolm W. Klein, eds. 1994. *Delinquent behavior among young people in the western world: First results of the international self-report delinquency study*. Amsterdam: Kugler Publications.

Kersten, Joachim. 2001. Groups of violent young males in Germany. In *The Eurogang paradox: Street gangs and youth groups in the U.S. and Europe*, edited by Malcolm W. Klein, Hans-Juergen Kerner, Cheryl L. Maxson, and Elmar G.M. Weitekamp. Dordrecht/Boston: Kluwer Academic Publishers.

Klein, Malcolm W. 1971. *Street gangs and street workers*. Englewood Cliffs, N.J.: Prentice-Hall.

Klein, Malcolm W. 1995. *The American street gang: Its nature, prevalence, and control*. Oxford, England: Oxford University Press.

Klein, Malcolm W. 2001. Street gangs: A cross-national perspective. In *Gangs in America*. 3rd ed., edited by C. Ronald Huff. Thousand Oaks, Calif.: Sage.

Klein, Malcolm W. 2004. *Gang cop: The words and ways of Officer Paco Domingo*. Walnut Creek, Calif.: AltaMira Press.

Klein, Malcolm W. 2005. The value of comparisons in street gang research. *Journal of Contemporary Criminal Justice* 21 (May): 135–142.

Klein, Malcolm W., Hans-Juergen Kerner, Cheryl L. Maxson, and Elmar G.M. Weitekamp, eds. 2001. *The Eurogang paradox: Street gangs and youth groups in the U.S. and Europe*. Dordrecht/Boston: Kluwer Academic Publishers.

Klein, Malcolm W., and Cheryl L. Maxson. 1994. Gangs and crack cocaine trafficking. In *Drugs and cocaine: Evaluating public policy initiatives*, edited by Doris L. Mackenzie and Craig Uchida. Thousand Oaks, Calif: Sage.

Klein, Malcolm W., and Cheryl L. Maxson. 2006. *Street gang patterns and policies*. Oxford, England: Oxford University Press.

Lien, Inger-Lise. 2001. The concept of honor, conflict, and violent behavior among youths in Oslo. In *The Eurogang paradox: Street gangs and youth groups in the U.S. and Europe*, edited by Malcolm W. Klein, Hans-Juergen Kerner, Cheryl L. Maxson, and Elmar G.M. Weitekamp. Dordrecht/Boston: Kluwer Academic Publishers.

Maxson, Cheryl L. 1993. Investigating gang migration: Contextual issues for intervention. *Gang Journal* 1, no. 2:1–8.

Maxson, Cheryl L. 1995. Street gangs and drug sales in two suburban cities. *Research in brief*. Washington, D.C.: National Institute of Justice.

Maxson, Cheryl L. 1998. *Gang members on the move*. Washington, D.C.: U.S. Department of Justice, Office of Juvenile Justice and Delinquency Prevention.

Maxson, Cheryl L., Karen Hennigan, and David C. Sloane. 2005. It's getting crazy out there: Can a civil gang injunction change a community? *Criminology and Public Policy* 4, no. 3:577–606.

Maxson, Cheryl L., and Malcolm W. Klein. 1990. Street gang violence: Twice as great or half as great? In *Gangs in America*, edited by C. Ronald Huff. Newbury Park, Calif.: Sage.

Maxson, Cheryl L. and Malcolm W. Klein. 1996. Defining gang homicide: An updated look at member and motive approaches. In *Gangs in America*. 2nd ed., edited by C. Ronald Huff. Thousand Oaks, Calif.: Sage.

Maxson, Cheryl L., and Malcolm W. Klein. 2002. "Play groups" no longer: Urban street gangs in the Los Angeles region. In *From Chicago to L.A.: Making sense of urban theory*, edited by Michael J. Dear. Thousand Oaks, Calif.: Sage.

McGarrell, Edmond F., and Steven Chermak. 2003. Problem solving to reduce gang and drug-related violence in Indianapolis. In *Policing gangs and youth violence*, edited by Scott H. Decker. Belmont, Calif.: Wadsworth.

Miller, Jody. 2001. *One of the guys: Girls, gangs, and gender*. New York: Oxford University Press.

Miller, Jody, Cheryl L. Maxson, and Malcolm W. Klein, eds. 2001. *The modern gang reader*. 2nd ed. Los Angeles: Roxbury Press.

Miller, Walter B. 1958. Inter-institutional conflict as a major impediment to delinquency prevention. *Human Organization* 17, no. 3:20–23.

Miller, Walter B. 1980. Gangs, groups and serious youth crime. In *Critical issues in juvenile delinquency*, edited by David Shichor and Delos H. Kelly. Lexington, Mass.: D.C. Heath.

Moore, Joan W. 1991. *Going down to the barrio: Homeboys and homegirls in change*. Philadelphia: Temple University Press.

Moore, Joan W., and James D. Vigil. 1989. Chicano gangs: Group norms and individual factors related to adult criminality. *Aztlan* 18:31.

National Youth Gang Center. 1999. *1996 national youth gang survey: Summary*. Washington, D.C.: U.S. Department of Justice, Office of Juvenile Justice and Delinquency Prevention.

Padilla, Felix M. 1992. *The gang as an American enterprise*. New Brunswick, N.J.: Rutgers University Press.

Salagaev, Alexander. 2001. Evolution of delinquent gangs in Russia. In *The Eurogang paradox: Street gangs and youth groups in the U.S. and Europe*, edited by Malcolm W. Klein, Hans-Juergen Kerner, Cheryl L. Maxson, and Elmar G.M. Weitekamp. Dordrecht/Boston: Kluwer Academic Publishers.

Sanchez-Jankowski, Martin. 1991. *Islands in the street: Gangs and American urban society*. Berkeley: University of California Press.

Sarnecki, Jerzy, and Tove Pettersson. 2001. Criminal networks in Sweden. In *The Eurogang paradox: Street gangs and youth groups in the U.S. and Europe*, edited by Malcolm W. Klein, Hans-Juergen Kerner, Cheryl L. Maxson, and Elmar G.M. Weitekamp. Dordrecht/Boston: Kluwer Academic Publishers.

Short, James F., Jr. 1996. *Gangs and adolescent violence*. Boulder: University of Colorado, Center for the Study and Prevention of Violence.

Short, James F., Jr., and Fred L. Strodtbeck. 1965. *Group process and gang delinquency*. Chicago: University of Chicago Press.

Snyder, Howard N., and Melissa Sickmund. 1999. *Juvenile offenders and victims: 1999 national report*. Washington, D.C.: U.S. Department of Justice, Office of Juvenile Justice and Delinquency Prevention.

Spergel, Irving A. 1966. *Street gang work: Theory and practice*. Reading, Mass.: Addison-Wesley.

Spergel, Irving A. 1995. *The youth gang problem: A community approach*. New York: Oxford University Press.

Thornberry, Terence P., Marvin D. Krohn, Alan J. Lizotte, Carolyn A. Smith, and Kimberly Tobin. 2003. *Gangs and delinquency in developmental perspective.* New York: Cambridge University Press.

Thrasher, Frederic M. 1927. *The gang: A study of 1313 gangs in Chicago.* Chicago: University of Chicago Press.

Valdez, Al. 2000. *Gangs: A guide to understanding street gangs.* San Clemente, Calif.: Law Tech Publishing.

Valdez, Avelardo, and Stephen Sifanek. 2004. "Getting high and getting by": Dimensions of drug selling behaviors among American Mexican gang members in South Texas. *Journal of Research in Crime and Delinquency* 41, no. 1:82–105.

Vigil, James D. 1988. *Barrio gangs: Street life and identity in Southern California.* Austin: University of Texas Press.

Vigil, James D. 2002. *A rainbow of gangs: Street cultures in the mega-city.* Austin: University of Texas Press.

Weitekamp, Elmar G.M. 2001. Gangs in Europe: Assessments at the millennium. In *The Eurogang paradox: Street gangs and youth groups in the U.S. and Europe*, edited by Malcolm W. Klein, Hans-Juergen Kerner, Cheryl L. Maxson, and Elmar G.M. Weitekamp. Dordrecht/Boston: Kluwer Academic Publishers.

Yablonsky, Lewis. 1963. *The violent gang.* New York: Macmillan.

INDEX